ST ANGELA'S PAR
148 8TH STREET
PACIFIC GROVE, CA 95950

idow's     lk

# Ronda Chervin

# A Widow's Walk

Encouragement, Comfort, and Wisdom
from the Widow-Saints

Our Sunday Visitor Publishing Division
Our Sunday Visitor, Inc.
Huntington, Indiana 46750

Unless otherwise indicated, Scripture quotations in this work are from the *Revised Standard Version Bible, Catholic Edition*, © 1965 and 1966 by the Division of Christian Education of the National Council of the Churches of Christ in the U.S.A., and used by permission of the copyright owner. The author and publisher are also grateful to other copyright holders whose materials appear in this volume and are cited in the Bibliography. If any copyrighted materials have been inadvertently used in this work without proper credit being given in one manner or another, please notify Our Sunday Visitor in writing so that future printings of this work may be corrected accordingly.

Copyright © 1998 by Our Sunday Visitor Publishing Division, Our Sunday Visitor, Inc.

All rights reserved. With the exception of short excerpts for critical reviews, no part of this book may be reproduced in any manner whatsoever without permission in writing from the publisher. Write:
Our Sunday Visitor Publishing Division
Our Sunday Visitor, Inc.
200 Noll Plaza
Huntington, Indiana 46750

International Standard Book Number: 0-87973-951-7
Library of Congress Catalog Card Number: 98-65865

Cover design by Tyler Ottinger

PRINTED IN THE UNITED STATES OF AMERICA

# Contents

# Introduction

Before telling you about the nature and purpose of *A Widow's Walk*, I want to tell you something about my own experience of widowhood.

## *Ronda's Widow Tale*

I became a widow at age fifty-six on October 9, 1993, when my husband, Martin Chervin, age seventy-four, died suddenly of cardiac arrest.

We were living at that time in Woodland Hills, California, in an extended family home with one of my twin daughters, Carla, her husband, Peter, and two of our little grandsons, Nicholas and Alexander.

The prospect of one day being a widow was not a new one for me. As a little girl I remember my mother and other relatives often remarking, while untangling the knots in my long tresses, that the V shape of the hair in the middle of my forehead was called a widow's peak. I guess this was a name based on some pointed headdress that widows wore at one time in history.

When marrying a man almost twenty years my senior, the possibility of becoming a widow one day was certainly part of my general awareness. This fear, however, was modified by the fact that my husband happened to be a man with incredible vitality and *joie de vivre*. We would always joke that, compared to him, I was the oldster, what with my sedentary professorial lifestyle.

When, only a few years after our marriage in 1962, my husband became disabled with a deadly form of asthma, the thought of death became a constant in our house. By 1968 my husband had become semi-disabled. He devoted himself no longer to his previous work as an international book salesman and instead spent the better part of each day doing wonderful original writing of such plays as *Born/Unborn* (a pro-life play about the evils of abortion), *Myself: Alma Mahler* (a one-woman show about the marriage of Alma and Gustav Mahler), and his recently published masterpiece, *Children of the Breath*[1] (about the part that Scripture doesn't tell us of the dialogue of Christ and Satan in the desert; see, for example, Matthew 4:1-11).

Every day of our life together, my husband had fantasies of the final fatal asthma attack and so did I. Was it surprising that I often thought about what I would do with myself after that seemingly always imminent death?

These fantasies rarely touched upon changes in my career life. Because my husband was too ill to support the family, I worked full-time all those years as a professor of Catholic philosophy. I loved my work and expected to continue it in one form or another until my own death.

The year Martin died, our children were all grown and we were enjoying our grandchildren. Our marriage was flourishing with a closeness we had not experienced since courtship. The reason for this renewal of our sacrament was, however, tragic. Our nineteen-year-old son had committed suicide in 1991. The agony for us of this fatal act drew us into much greater emotional and spiritual intimacy than we had ever experienced. An account of this period in my life can be found in my book *En Route to Eternity — The Story of My Life*,[2] published by Miriam Press.

The fantasies I nourished throughout my married life had to do with two other areas: holiness and second husbands! To start with the holiness aspect, it was my conviction that my husband, Martin, was an obstacle to my holiness. Even though he had converted to the Catholic faith, as I had, his idea was that religion could be a most important part of life, but not the be-all and end-all. On the contrary, in spite of my terrible faults, such as raging anger even about trifles, I had always been convinced that all Christians were called to be as holy as saints.

In my daydreams, Martin's death would mean that I would no longer have to compromise with his somewhat luxurious ideas about lifestyle, including the purchase of myriad gadgets and the enjoyment of cruises and similar activities. Once alone, able to make my own decisions, I would become a true daughter of Saint Francis of Assisi. In moments of anger about my husband's insistence that all the goods of the earth were set aside by God before his birth to bring him joy, I would picture how, after his death, all the hated expensive items in the house could be lavishly distributed to the poor from my bountiful hands.

After this giving-away party, I would be free to live in utter simplicity, without a car, walking everywhere, going to jail for Operation Rescue if I wished, and, of course, with a prayer life as focused as that of Saint Teresa of Ávila.

In a somewhat opposite manner, my fantasies about being a widow ranged over the field of how different men, presently bachelor friends of the family, would waste not an hour after the funeral telling me of their undying love and sweeping me off my feet into a glorious engagement and perfect marriage.

The reason I am including more about this aspect of my life than you might expect, even though it is humiliating to recount, is that I hope this book might attract some readers who would otherwise not be able to relate to this situation. There are beautiful books about widowhood such as *By Grief Refined*, written by my dear friend Alice Von Hildebrand, which show how to lift up to Christ the unbearable grief that comes with the loss of a marriage as perfect as is possible on this earth. I was much inspired by reading her book. But given the complexities of my own marriage, her advice did not always apply to my situation. My thought, therefore, is that through my detailing the absurd antics of my early widowhood, the way the widow-saints helped me out of this will be more credible.

So, in my daydreams before my husband's death, those bachelor friends became instantly converted from all their faults by the terrific influence of my saintly companionship. At times of sadness or boredom, I would embroider these fantasies, planning every detail of conversation and future.

Not one to waste time, I indeed started to try to turn fantasy into reality immediately after my husband's sudden death. Before telling you some of the funny things that happened in the process, I should relate that my feelings at the time of his actual death were quite different from what I had imagined beforehand.

Because of the ambiguities of our marriage, I had always been afraid that I might not be able to act as expected at the moment of his death. That was not true. Not only did I wail with grief, but I even reverted to a biblical archetype, rending my dress by tearing the hem in two as I rocked on the living room floor holding my daughters in my arms.

The feeling during the first week was not liberation; instead, it was a peculiar, scary lightness. I described it as floating on the ceiling like a balloon released from a rock to which it had been tied. The dizzy vertigo of that time was still with me two and a half years into widowhood. What I realized is that my earthy husband was the ground for my feet. Without him I did not soar toward Christ: I just floated, miserable and without ballast! The fact that we were living twenty minutes from the epicenter of the big L.A. earthquake that struck but three months afterward only intensified the feeling of shakiness. At the worst moments, since Martin's death, this lack of grounding took the form of severe anxiety attacks, sometimes several a day at anniversaries and holidays, as well as chronic depression.

Because of my active fantasy life, I absolutely hadn't the faintest idea of how horrible being a widow could be.

Concerning the "instant holiness" daydream, I did enjoy enormously giving lots of money away to family and friends. Lots of property left the house even before the funeral. I was also now able to give away large sums of money to the poor out of my salary.

However, to my horror I discovered that this joy was not a permanent thing. Yes, I felt happy writing checks and giving things away, but how long could each of these peaks last? In the meantime, the loss of my husband gnawed at me and was making me utterly miserable every other minute of each day!

Moreover, the unholy faults of my nature didn't go away, such as chronic anger about large and small frustrations, manic talkativeness, and so on.

Meanwhile my prayer life, which had gone into a sort of dark night after the death of my son, moved only to gray, with one or two beautiful moments each day, but certainly not into the glowing radiance I had imagined in my hopes for my single life of contemplative glory!

On the romantic side, I went through about five immediate rejections and about seven more over the next two and a half years involving men who would simply run like hell when they found out I was available not as a friend but as a potential spouse!

It is fun to write about these encounters with humor, but actually in many of these cases I felt terrible pain, believing that each rejection was proof that I was a hideous old bag, garrulous, annoying, and generally impossible to view as an object of romantic love. No amount of loving praise and comforting reassurances from family and friends seemed to heal these feelings that got worse and worse as each attempt ended in failure.

Running parallel with my search for a second husband — a pursuit I like to describe as akin to a barracuda looking for prey — was a more holy but equally, so far, frustrating attempt to become part of some utopian Catholic community or to become a late-vocation nun. In each case there was something about the group that made it clearly unsuitable for a woman of my personality.

I did have an absolutely beautiful moment in prayer during which Jesus appeared to me in an inner vision in the form of El Greco's image of Christ in bridegroom garb. He told me that I belonged to him. I asked him if he wanted me to join a particular order of Sisters. He seemed to say: "Yes, that way you can focus on me alone." I was ecstatic about this; but my mentors all cautioned me, and, in fact, when I was with some aspirants of this order I felt not peaceful and good but claustrophobic.

In a manner I would never have predicted, the issue of my future was mirrored in my clothing. When bent on the barracuda search for men I wore lipstick (I hadn't worn it since I was a teenager) and my most colorful clothing. When dreaming instead of the consecrated life, I dropped the makeup and wore various plain blue outfits I had sewn by hand in fits of eagerness for a new identity as a pseudo-nun. In the middle of the day, if my fantasies changed, I would feel the need to immediately remove the dull blue dresses, or vice-versa, to rub off the lipstick quickly and put my long flowing hair up in a bun!

As I was somewhat manic-depressive and also extremely open in conversing about my thoughts and decisions, my friends began to look forward to seeing me, primarily to learn of the latest episode in my spiritual soap opera.

Basically my feeling is that all along I undervalued the deep love my husband had for me, discounted the way his virtues sustained me, and could not guess how painful the loneliness of the single life really is, even with wonderful friends surrounding me at every turn.

At the point of doing this book, I am calmer. I am living with my daughter and family in Arizona, with frequent visits to my other daughter and family in California, pursuing a life of prayer, writing, speaking, running workshops and retreats, and administering an adult-education program at Saint John Vianney parish in Sedona, while helping at home with family needs such as dishwashing, laundry, and taking the kiddies for walks. At this time I have decided to stop looking at communities; instead I have started a movement with a dedicated way of life, including plain blue garb for those with private vows (including myself).

During this turbulent period, I realized that one of my greatest needs was to research the widow-saints to see what wisdom and comfort they could provide for me as a frenetic but devout widow. Will their example lead me to committing myself to being a consecrated woman, renouncing dreams of finding a second husband forever? Or will studying their lives reconcile me to being a single woman, open to any future God wants to gift me with? In any case I hope to seek Christ no longer as an escape from the trials of daily life, or simply as fuel for an activist life, but instead as the true center of my heart: my Second Bridegroom.

## Our Widow Tale and the Widow-Saints

A word about the format, or structure, of *A Widow's Walk*. My book is designed to trace Christ's way of love for widows, generally based on the data gleaned from reading the lives and writings of the widow-saints. My purpose is to find comfort and wisdom for myself and also to minister to other widows.

Accordingly the first part of *A Widow's Walk* is divided into phases of the widow's journey, matched with narratives and quotations from the saints. You will learn about happily and unhappily married saints, how they experienced the crisis of widowhood. You will see how they managed with their children, with new financial problems, and with other concerns.

You will find some receiving help from relatives and others finding friends and relatives to be obstacles to the new directions they were seeking. In considering the role of the Church community in the new life of the widow-saints, I will present narratives about spiritual friends and advisers who sustained these women in sometimes extraordinary ways. I will present a summary of what we know about widows in Scripture. You will be able to identify, perhaps, with the way some holy widows encountered Christ even more deeply in the Mass and in Holy Communion. Certainly when we are brought low in vulnerability we appreciate even more how much we need to rely on the Mystical Body of Christ in the sacraments and in the faith of our brothers and sisters to sustain us.

The second part (entitled "Widow Roles — The Saints Show the Way") goes into different choices that each widow can make concerning her own future ministry in the Church. In each part, or chapter, of the book we will study the way one or two widow-saints witnessed to Christ working through them in such ministries as care of the needy (including family), penitential prayer, prophetic heroism, contemplative interior absorption in the life of the Trinity, becoming a consecrated woman, or founding a community.

I will then move into sharing the stories of widow-saints who tell us more particularly about their experience of Christ as the Bridegroom of their hearts, souls, and even bodies.

The last chapter depicts Mary as the exalted widow

— our exemplar, sister, and mother, as we seek to become the holy widows we believe God wants us to be.

* * *

Before entering into the particular choices that we and our saintly sisters make as widows, I need to clarify a few points about my reasons for researching the particular widow-saints you will be reading about.

First of all, the list that will follow is not complete. It consists of widow-saints and holy women I happen to know about from my own studies during and after the time I was writing my *Treasury of Women Saints* and *Prayers of the Women Mystics*, both published by Servant Publications. In the case of holy widows whose lives I have not only referred to but written about in detail, under various headings, I have tried as much as possible to choose saints whose writings are available so that you can read their actual words about their experiences. You will find some material that is repeated more than once to make a point, although not in the exact same words.

Not all the women described in this book have been formally canonized, but all have been considered to be saints and most are in the process of being evaluated positively under this title. I have included only women who were married at the time of their widowhood. This is because it seems to me that divorced women whose ex-husbands die afterward have different traumas, wounds, and problems.

To turn to another consideration, you will be interested to know that there is a certain stereotype of the widow-saint that my research so far has proven to be mistaken. According to the popular image, most holy widows were unhappily married women who longed all their lives to be consecrated and who rushed immediately after the death of their spouses into the convent.

It is true that many of the widow-saints do fit this

15

pattern, but there are quite a number who do not. Some were very content in their marriages, and some who later became nuns, Sisters, or Third Order celibates thought long and hard before making this choice.

Many Catholics also believe that if a widow does remarry, this is proof that she is not holy. I do not think that such a conclusion is valid. While it is sometimes part of the holiness of a consecrated woman that she has sacrificed marriage, this does not mean that marriage or remarriage need be a barrier to holiness. Since most canonization procedures in modern times have as their starting point the desire of men and women in particular orders to see their founder or foundress recognized as holy, we simply know much more about holy men and women in the consecrated life than holy laypeople.

Nonetheless, I found I could not help but be struck by how many of the widow-saints did reject even the possibility of remarriage in favor of a publicly or privately consecrated vow, following in this choice the preponderance of advice for widows to be found in Scripture.

I am appending to these introductory remarks a list of the widow-saints I have become acquainted with, whether in passing or in a fairly detailed manner. If I have missed your favorite, please write me a note about where to find out about her for a second edition.

Widow-saints included or mentioned in this work (in alphabetical order) are:

Saint Adelaide (931-999)

Blessed Angela of Foligno (1248-1309)

Blessed Angeline Corbara (died 1377)

Saint Brigid (also called Bridget, Birgitta, or Brigitta) of Sweden (1323-1373)

Saint Catherine of Genoa (1447-1510)

Blessed Clare of Rimini (1282-1346)

Saint Clotilda (474-545)

Concepción (Conchita) Cabrera de Armida (1862-1937)

Blessed Dorothy of Mantua (1347-1394)

Saint Elizabeth of Hungary (1207-1231)

Saint Elizabeth of Portugal (1271-1336)

Saint Elizabeth Seton (1774-1821)

Saint Ethelreda (or Audrey) (died 679)

Saint Frances of Rome (1384-1440)

Blessed Humiliana Cerchi (1216-1246)

Saint Jane (or Jeanne) de Chantal (1572-1641)

Blessed Jane (or Jeanne) de Maille (1332-1414)

Saint Jeanne de Lestonnac (died 1640)

Saint Joaquina (1783-1854)

Saint Jutta (died 1260)

Blessed Louise Albertoni (1474-1533)

Saint Louise de Marillac (1591-1660)

Blessed Marie Marguerite d'Youville (1701-1771)

Blessed Maria Domenica Brun Barbantini (1789-1868)

Mother María Luisa Josefa of the Blessed Sacrament (1866-1937)

Blessed Marie of the Incarnation (Acarie) (1566-1618)*

Blessed Marie of the Incarnation (Martin) (1599-1672)

Saint Matilda (895-968)

Blessed Michelina of Pesaro (1300-1356)

Saint Monica (331-387)

Saint Paula (347-404)

Praxedes Fernandez (died 1936)

Saint Rita of Cascia (1381-1457)

* * *

Here is my prayer as I close this introduction: "My Jesus, you allowed as part of your plan for me and for

---

* All references to Blessed Marie of the Incarnation in this work are to Martin and not Acarie, who is mentioned here only as a widow-saint the reader might be interested in learning more about through another source.

my sister-widows that we would go through this particular form of anguish in all its forms. But your wish is not that we should die of anxiety, depression, or despair, but that we should receive your love as a second bridegroom in such a way that, like the widow-saints, we may be joyful in the midst of suffering and true sisters to everyone we meet. By means of meditating on the themes in this treatise, may we truly reach your goal for us."

# The Widow's Plight — Ours and the Saints'

## A Happy or Unhappy Marriage?

In reporting about the marriages of the widow-saints before they lost their spouses, I have limited myself to simply summarizing whether their time as wives were happy or unhappy, except in the case of especially featured widows.

In some important cases it should be noted that a woman was forced to marry against her will but that the marriage eventually became happy because of the holiness of the wife.

More will be found about most of these saints in other chapters, but for now I want to list some who were reluctant to enter into the marriage either because they wished they could have been consecrated to Christ as his spouse, or because they rejected a particular suitor: Blessed Humiliana Cerchi, Blessed Angeline Corbara, Saint Brigid of Sweden, Saint Rita of Cascia, and Blessed Louise Albertoni.

Among the happily married we can count the Virgin Mary (wife of Saint Joseph), Saint Paula, Saint Clotilda, Saint Matilda, Saint Jutta, Saint Elizabeth of Hungary, Saint Brigid of Sweden, Blessed Jane de Maille (who had a celibate marriage with her first husband), Saint Frances of Rome, Saint Catherine of Genoa (whose husband agreed to a celibate marriage after her conversion), Saint Jane de Chantal, Saint Jeanne de Lestonnac, Blessed Louise Albertoni, Saint Louise de Marillac, Saint

Joaquina, Saint Elizabeth Seton, and Concepción (Conchita) Cabrera de Armida.

Among the saints who were known to be especially happy with their spouses we can point to Saint Elizabeth of Hungary, who was so attached to her devout husband that, even when praying on her knees during the night, she held his hand in hers.

Saint Frances of Rome (1384-1440) was so happily married that it is said there was never a single dispute between wife and husband.[1] After many family tragedies, when the children were grown up, Lorenzo, the husband of Frances, agreed to renounce their sexual life together so that his saintly wife would be free to start a congregation of Benedictine Sisters, which she herself entered after his death.

In the journals of Conchita — the Mexican holy woman and a grandmother, about whom you will learn more as you continue reading — we find an articulate expression of why she thought that a happy marriage was a supernatural vocation. Conchita was extremely religious as a girl but longed to be married and have children. "Lord, I feel so unable to love you, so I want to get married. Give me many children so that they will love you better than I," she would pray.[2]

In those days engagements lasted a long time. Conchita was engaged for about nine years, from the age of thirteen until she was twenty-two. She tried always to love her fiancé not in an exclusively natural way but rather to love him in God.[3] She saw no conflict between love of God and love for her Pancho. When forced by the customs of the time to attend fancy balls and theatrical performances, Conchita wore a hair shirt under her fashionable clothing.

Conchita describes her husband as always respectful and tender, a model husband and father. She continually arranged things in the home to make him happy to be there after work and delighted him with the gifts and games that she devised. During retreats she made plans for helping him in his business, for being kind to all his family, some of whom were not very charitable to her.[4]

There is a charming story about the marriage of another Mexican holy woman, Mother María Luisa Josefa of the Blessed Sacrament (1866-1937), foundress of the Discalced Carmelite Sisters of the Third Order. On her wedding day, this woman made a visit to the Carmelites and asked to be admitted to the convent. Apparently she was so naïve she didn't realize that marriage was an impediment to a religious vocation. Naturally when she introduced the bridegroom, she was informed of her error.

You will read more about the happy marriages of other women saints when I describe their lives in other parts of this book.

There are also many instances of unhappy marriages among the women saints, including those of Saint Monica (whose husband, a pagan most of his life, was a worldly, ill-tempered man), Blessed Humiliana Cerchi (whose husband was not religious, was very miserly, and converted only on his deathbed, thanks in part to Humiliana's uncomplaining kindness), Saint Elizabeth of Portugal (whose royal husband was dissolute and jealous), Blessed Dorothy of Mantua, Saint Rita of Cascia, Blessed Marie Marguerite d'Youville (who will simply be referred to as Marguerite instead of Marie Marguerite from here on), and Praxedes (pronounced *Prahk-SAY-dehz*) Fernandez.

Of these the most famous unhappy marriage was that of Saint Rita of Cascia.[5] As you will see when you read about this widow-saint in another chapter, Rita was married to one of the worst men in the history of Catholic hagiography. Her husband, Paul, was hypercritical, violent with everyone including his meek wife, alcoholic, and probably unfaithful. Through her prayers and penances and the grace of God, he was converted to a virtuous way of life and died as a good Christian.

Some people think that anyone who chooses to marry a brutal man must have had a psychologically disordered childhood. Even if this may often be the case, the strange story of Blessed Marguerite d'Youville, who died in 1771, shows that it is not always the case. Our eighteenth-century Canadian saint had one of the happiest early childhoods possible.[6]

Marguerite Dufrost de la Jemmerais was one of six children born in Quebec, Canada, to parents of French ancestry. As a girl, Marguerite spent most of her time helping her mother with the care of her younger siblings. Even though the comfortable farming family was brought low by the death of her father, they lived as best they could off the land. Sent off at age eleven, as was the custom, to an Ursuline convent school, the girl showed herself to be unusually bright and of a peaceful nature. It was there that Marguerite learned devotion to the Sacred Heart.

Even though she was attracted to the religious life, she assumed she would marry one day. She was quite willing to be married to the man her family picked for her, François d'Youville, who happened to be handsome and wealthy.[7] Unfortunately the marriage turned out tragically.

François was often gone on trading expeditions that turned out to involve bribing the Indians to give up valuable furs for "fire water," a practice that contributed to his undoing before Marguerite turned him around.

Equally difficult was Marguerite's domestic situation. She expected to be "at least second mistress" in the home of her husband and mother-in-law. "She had rich experience in homemaking"[8] and expected to make use of it in a creative manner. Instead the young woman found herself completely under the domination of a bitter, jealous mother-in-law who resented the beauty, charm, and refined virtues of her son's wife.

Marguerite's husband soon showed himself to be crude, selfish, and indifferent.[9] She wept bitter tears when she realized how difficult her situation was to be. She made up her mind never to criticize him even though his behavior became more and more ignoble. He liked to leave for long periods of time without explanation, and even stayed away at the time of the birth of their first child. He was too busy trading liquor for furs.

There are records of a delegation of Indians appealing to the governor-general of Montreal that "Youville . . . gets us drunk every day, and makes us drink up the value of all our furs, so that we are miserable and naked, without even shirts or clothes of any kind to cover us, or firearms to hunt with."[10] The natives especially regretted that these temptations led them away from the prayers and spiritual exercises they were being taught by the good missionaries.

Since her husband was gone most of the time, the disgust of the people of Montreal at his business practices was taken out on Marguerite, who had to put up with the townspeople's sneers and reproaches when she stepped out with her baby to go to the marketplace.[11] Desperately Marguerite tried by prayer and example to convert her husband, lest his soul be damned for eternity.

To these sufferings was added the misery of the death of her baby son. She gave the male child born next the same name, her husband's, probably imagining that this would soften his heart to take an interest in his family. Her husband was also absent for this boy's birth and baptism.[12] Then came a little girl, Marie, who also died as a baby. There followed Louise, who lived less than three months!

After the death of his mother, François gave himself up to a completely dissipated life of drinking, carousing, and gambling. He squandered all the family money, leaving Marguerite to work hard to provide for necessities.

To be able to endure the harsh circumstances of her life, the future saint took solace in joining the Confraternity of the Holy Family, in this way taking as her own the family of Jesus, Mary, and Joseph. Under the guidance of a fine priest she learned how to sanctify the pain of her life day by day. The priest predicted that God would accomplish a great work through her one day.

A fifth child, Charles (who would eventually become a priest), came during this time when Marguerite was still mourning the loss of three children.

Marguerite became a widow when her husband died suddenly from inflammation of the lungs. She requested that the priests of the Church offer three hundred sixty Masses for his soul. In spite of his abusive behavior she grieved his death, carrying a sixth child, who also was to die as a baby. The mother was left with two children — one aged six and the other a baby; she was also destitute and burdened with debts.[13]

More of the story of this woman whom no amount of heartache and tragedy could overcome will be found in subsequent sections of this book.

We will now take a look at Praxedes Fernandez, who died in 1936. She was a Spanish holy woman who was fond of her husband when she married him but found him to be an irritable person, not above striking her when she annoyed him by her piety. He also liked to spend long evenings with friends in taverns rather than with her and their children.

Parenthetically, you might want to know that there are canonized saints who were sinners before, during, or after their marriages, that is, before their conversions. We can include in this category Blessed Clare of Rimini,

Blessed Angela of Foligno, Blessed Michelina of Pesaro, and somewhat less extravagantly Saint Catherine of Genoa.

Are you skeptical? Read more and you will be astounded at what the grace of God can do.

Blessed Clare of Rimini, one of several sinner-widows who became widow-saints, was born in 1282 into a wealthy family and was married early. She lost both her husband and parents when still young. Being a vivacious young woman, she yielded to temptation and gave herself to a life of fun to the point of indulging in sin. Clare remarried but still indulged in scandalous friendships. One day she heard a voice in church telling her to give up sin. She underwent a complete conversion, took the habit of the Third Order of Saint Francis, and started a life of penance.

Widowed again, she continued even more fervently in her penances by sleeping on the ground, eating only bread and water, and praying most of the night. Blessed Clare of Rimini took care of the poor, begging for what they needed if she didn't have enough. She was a peacemaker in families, and Clare had to endure persecution for her zeal. Before her death in 1346 she had formed some other women into a community of the rule of Saint Clare of Assisi.

I want to end these few pages about widows whose marriages were unusual with a short account of the ups and downs in the spousal life of Saint Catherine of Genoa, who died in 1510. Information about this famous Italian saint comes from the book *Saint Catherine of Genoa: Life and Sayings*.[14]

Born to a wealthy, powerful family of Genoa, Catherine was a very religious young girl, devoted especially to the passion of Christ. She tried to enter a convent but was refused because she was only thirteen. She was married at the age of sixteen to one Giuliano Adorni, a man for whom she felt only repugnance. He was much older, and the match was arranged by the families for political reasons. The marriage was very unhappy. Giuliano was a man of strange and dissolute ways.[15] He also squandered her fortune as well as his own. She felt abandoned by her husband and was lonely, melancholy, and unloved. She lived literally incarcerated in her home most of the day except for going to Mass.

For five years the young attractive woman sought distraction from her despair in the enjoyment of worldly vanities. In her early middle age, Catherine had an over-whelming religious experience that changed her life to-tally.

Here is an account of this happening: Catherine's sister, who was a nun, persuaded her to go to confession. When she knelt down before the priest, who was a saintly man, her heart was pierced by such tremendous love of God that she almost fainted. She was so purified by this instance of grace that she decided to spurn all worldliness and sin. Once back at home, Catherine went to a private room. Overwhelmed by the love of God for her, she sighed deeply for her sins. She had an inner vision of Christ on the cross dripping with blood. At that time she became a daily communicant, which was very rare in those times. She suffered terribly if she thought she might be deprived of this food for her soul.

After three years of Catherine's penance and ministry to the poor and sick, accompanied by ecstatic mystical experiences, her husband became reconciled with her and agreed to live with her in a celibate life like brother and sister. The pair moved to a house in the poor district of town and devoted themselves to the care of the sick.

When Catherine was fifty years old, her husband died of a long and painful illness, thankfully at peace with God. She lived for about fifteen years after his death.

While we are summarizing facts about our variety of

widow-saints, you might find it interesting that while many of the widows were older women (by the contemporary definition of old in their times), many were very young or fairly young, including Blessed Humiliana Cerchi, Saint Elizabeth of Hungary, Blessed Angeline Corbara, Blessed Clare of Rimini, Blessed Michelina of Pesaro, Saint Jane de Chantal, and Blessed Marie of the Incarnation.

## *Grieving*

You have sent me misery and hardship,
but you will give me life again,
you will pull me up again from the depths of the earth,
prolong my old age, and once more comfort me.

— Psalm 71:20-21 *(The Jerusalem Bible)*

I wonder how many women have derived consolation, as I have, from reading this Psalm as we make the painful journey from marriage to widowhood.

Even in the case of women who thought widowhood might be a liberation from a wretched marital situation or a way to pursue holiness without encumbrances coming from the worldly goals of their husbands, there is often much grief.

A most startling story of ambivalence in the crisis of widowhood can be found in the words of Blessed Angela of Foligno (1248-1309), a Franciscan Italian mystic. You may wish to start with her life story in "Widow Roles — The Saints Show the Way," the chapter about widow-saints who were intercessors, penitents, and pilgrims, before reading this particular section about her experience of the new life alone.

Blessed Angela had been a sinful married woman. It is unclear if her infidelities went as far as outright adultery, but the implication in what she dictated to the priest, who was her confessor and scribe, is that her sins were mortal, that is, deadly to her soul (for non-Catholic readers who are not familiar with the term "mortal sin").

Describing the time after her conversion, but before her widowhood, when Angela was eager to live for Christ alone but frustrated by the worldliness of her mother, husband, and sons, she says, in the book that is now called *Angela of Foligno: Complete Works*: "At that time my mother, who had been a great obstacle to me, died. In like manner my husband died, as did all my sons in a short space of time. Because I had already entered the aforesaid way, and had prayed to God for their death, I felt a great consolation when it happened . . . since God had conceded me this aforesaid favor, my heart would always be within God's heart, and God's heart always within me."[16]

It should be noted, however, that later on, in the part of her book that is called the "Memorial," she spoke of the great pain caused by the death of her mother and sons.[17]

By contrast, Saint Elizabeth of Hungary, who was so happily married, wept bitterly for days when Ludwig (Louis) died.

Saint Jane de Chantal was prostrate for four months with grief over the death of her husband in an accident. She had great difficulty forgiving the hunter who shot her husband, even though it was the result of a freak accident in which the man mistook Jane's husband for an animal he was hunting in the forest.

As for Saint Elizabeth Seton, this is what she wrote a friend a few months after her spouse's death: "I have been to my dear [husband's] grave and wept plentifully over it with the unrestrained affection which the last sufferings of his life, added to remembrance of former years, had made almost more than precious — when you read my daily memorandums since I left home you will feel what my love has been, and acknowledge that

God alone could. . . ."[18] (The rest of the sentence is missing because of a torn page at this point in Elizabeth's manuscript.)

She writes about visiting a museum and loving the masterpieces of art but also feeling "alone but half enjoyed" herself, since she missed so much the joy her husband would have had in pointing things out to her.[19] After one excursion she wrote to this same friend: "My poor heart was in the clouds roving after my Williams soul and repeating my God you are my God, and so I am now alone in the world with you and my little ones, but you are my Father and doubly theirs."[20] (Incidentally, the editors of *Selected Writings from the Journal and Letters of Elizabeth Seton* have apparently opted to ignore a number of spelling and punctuation errors or inconsistencies as well as some capitalizations evidently customary at that time. These inconsistencies, etc., will be found throughout the writings of Saint Elizabeth as well as in some other works quoted in this book.)

It is a well-known part of grieving to be extremely fatigued. This is expressed by Elizabeth Seton, writing of the time when she was living alone with her five small children: "My woman [servant] has been again sick these five days I have been deprived of the dear morning visit of my Master — on Sunday I was so weak as not to be able to walk to town with my other fatigues. . . ."[21]

The husband of Conchita of Mexico died after they had been married for sixteen years and had parented nine children, one of whom died when he was six years old.

Here is how she describes the days just before his death: "What struggles . . . what pains . . . what sufferings! This sword pierced my soul, without any assuagement, without any consolation. . . . Oh! If I had not been sustained by Him, then through my great weakness, I would have succumbed! I saw, I affirmed, moment by moment, that my husband was losing his life . . . my heart was torn with pain. . . . To the measure that I saw our separation approaching, the tenderness of my heart toward him took on more and more considerable proportions. I felt I had no longer head, nor faith, nor reason, but only a heart. I experienced, as it were, horror for the spiritual life. What days I spent! What hours! What nights!"[22]

Like Elizabeth Seton, she was ever at her husband's deathbed preparing him for eternity. After his death Conchita describes a visit to the cemetery on her husband's birthday. Many widows find these previously festive anniversaries especially painful.

"What a sad day for my heart, the heart of a wife and mother," Conchita relates, "was this day, my husband's birthday. . . . Overcoming my feelings, I went to his tomb with my children to spend the morning there, right near his remains, praying and weeping . . . I recalled at that time how Jesus wept over Lazarus . . . death is something terrible. . . . My children's and my own tears moistened this soil . . . then there passed through my imagination, in rapid flight, the years gone by and memories of them: sorrows, joys and dreams. In an instant all had vanished, like smoke at the breath of death. . . . Oh! how ephemeral is life! . . . What do we do when this time is not employed for God alone?"[23]

Many widows find that they get a much clearer picture of all their husband's virtues after death strips away the images of daily life that are neutral or mixed with the flaws of the same man.

Did Conchita find a bittersweet solace in drawing this portrait of her husband in her diary?

"Here is a picture of what my husband was. He was very good, a Christian and a gentleman, honest, correct, intelligent and big-hearted. He was sensitive to adversity, full of tenderness toward me, an excellent father of a family, who had no other diversion than his children. They were his joy and he suffered greatly when they were ill . . . a homebody, very simple, filled with deference and delicacy. He had a strong, energetic character, which, as time passed, he toned down . . . from the day after our wedding until his death, he let me receive Communion every day . . . he had a great fear of death . . . before dying, he made a general confession and his fear of death changed into perfect acceptance of the divine will."[24]

So terrible was her grief during the first days of widowhood that the doctors thought she would die of it. "Even when I control myself," she wrote, "I go through moments of despondency. My tears flow very often without my being able to hold them back. My heart of flesh recalls many a sorrowful memory. I suffer, drinking deep of sorrow. May God be blessed for all! . . . The sound of my children crying over their father pierced my soul. . . . My body is exhausted. Now it is that I feel wearied. . . . May the Lord sustain me with His cross."[25]

On the third anniversary of her husband's death Conchita wrote in her diary that "my heart struggles constantly. Truly, and literally, I water with my tears the bread I eat, the ground and my crucifix! Oh my Jesus! What You wish, that I wish too. . . . I feel so awfully alone. Oh Mary, my Mother, have pity on me."[26]

After twenty years, and then thirty years, she was praying constantly that Christ would fill her husband with his glory and "greet him for me."[27]

## Remarriage?

As Alice Von Hildebrand explains in *By Grief Refined*, her beautiful book about widowhood, when a marriage is the consummation of a spousal love in Christ, focused on the unique preciousness of the beloved, there is, naturally, a repugnance to the idea of remarriage. On the other hand, she realizes that in many marriages entered into for the motive of love, there may still be an imperfect union of hearts for many reasons. In those cases, the possibility of remarriage may seem desirable. Then, again, there can be reasons for seeking remarriage that involve the legitimate needs of the children.[28]

In the case of the widow-saints, the motives for their first marriages were varied. Often, in the past, marriages were arranged with only a minimal assent on the part of the young women to be espoused. As mentioned earlier, in many cases the desire to be a consecrated woman was thwarted by parental insistence on marriage, often for economic reasons — or political ones in the case of royalty.

The decision of Saint Jane de Chantal is interesting for us because it includes so many of the elements so far described. There is no doubt whatsoever that Jane loved her husband deeply. Shortly after the death of her husband she made a private vow of consecration. Nonetheless, in spite of her desire for holiness, she did fight with temptations to remarry. When we find out her circumstances it is easy to understand why she wavered. In those days in France, apparently, an upper-class widow in Jane's legal situation would lose the right to all her husband's goods and also her children would be disinherited, unless she moved into the house of someone in her husband's family.

Jane's father-in-law, who was eager to make use of her great talents for household management, insisted that she come to live in his manor house even though he was keeping a mistress and the domain included offspring of this liaison.

Since some of her children were still young, Jane could not enter the convent for many years. The only way she could escape from her father-in-law's house was by remarriage to one of the wealthy suitors who were seeking her hand.

During one of the first times that Saint Francis de Sales met Jane at a social gathering, he chided her mildly for still wearing a garb that suggested she was open to remarriage even though she had told him about her private vow.

You will read more about Jane's decisions later on in this book. But this will suffice to show how even a happily married woman might feel remarriage was a path to consider seriously.

Saint Jane's ambivalence may comfort widow-readers who may go through any number of years of uncertainty not only about availability of possible second husbands but also about their own deepest wishes.

It is recounted that even though Saint Louise de Marillac (1591-1660) had no wish to remarry, she found her early widowhood lonely and depressing. Her self-chosen solitude in her decision to remove herself from the social frivolities of the Parisian court after her husband died increased feelings of sinfulness about not having chosen the religious life before her marriage. Of course, God had his own plan and would eventually fill her days with constant work in the founding of the Sisters of Charity.

By contrast, Conchita wrote in her diary that just before her husband died, with "my forehead resting on the forehead of him who was so good to me, I consecrated myself to God to be all for Him."[29] She never wavered in this decision; yet, after her children were grown, she described the last part of her life, from 1917 until she died in 1937, as a time of painful solitude.[30]

Saint Elizabeth Seton loved her husband dearly. Her great wish, after his death and her own conversion to the Roman Catholic faith, was to be a religious Sister in some way consonant with mothering her five young children. Yet when she met an ardent Catholic man in her travels who seemed to understand her, she felt drawn to him and had to struggle to overcome the desire to re-marry in the light of her higher calling. She described herself as having an inflammable heart.

Years later Elizabeth, hearing about a widow-friend who was considering remarriage, advised that she should stay single. The reason she gave was that even in the best of marriages the adjustment of one personality to the other is so difficult that it was better to be alone!

Whereas Blessed Clare of Rimini remarried *of her own will*, and was twice widowed, sometimes relatives of the women saints put pressure on the widow to remarry against her will. Blessed Humiliana Cerchi, who died in 1246, resisted this pressure successfully as did Blessed Jane de Maille.

Here are some stories of earlier centuries that illustrate what unusual combinations of circumstances might influence holy widows to remarry under such pressure.

Saint Ethelreda (or Etheldreda, as it is also spelled), who lived in England and died in 679, was also known as Audrey. She lived with her first husband like a sister rather than a wife. After his death, her relatives insisted she marry Egfrid, king of Northumbria. Since he was but a boy, he agreed to a continent (that is, nonsexual) marriage; but when he grew older he wanted a "real" wife, so the Church authorities suggested that Ethelreda become a nun. She founded a double monastery at Ely.[31]

Equally intriguing is the story of Saint Adelaide. This princess of Burgundy[32] was betrothed at a tender age (two, to be exact!) to Lothaire, who would become king of Italy. Her husband was assassinated shortly after the wedding. The enemies of her husband wanted her to re-marry into their family. She refused. They brutalized her and kept her in near solitary confinement in the castle. She was saved by a priest who dug a passage out for her. She hid in the forest until she was rescued. When Otto of Germany invaded Italy he insisted on marrying

Adelaide to consolidate his power. They bore five children. Widowed again, she left for Vienna to escape the resentment of her daughter-in-law. Finally she herself became the regent of Italy. She was revered for forgiving her enemies, founding monasteries, and attempting to convert pagans. She died at age sixty-eight in the year 999.

## *Single-Parenting or Aloneness*

I was surprised to find how many of the widow-saints journeyed toward holiness not on a solitary road but accompanied for quite a distance by their children.

Some of these widow-saints include Blessed Michelina of Pesaro, Saint Rita of Cascia, Saint Brigid of Sweden, Saint Jeanne de Lestonnac, Saint Jane de Chantal, Saint Louise de Marillac, Blessed Marie of the Incarnation, Blessed Marguerite d'Youville, Saint Joaquina, Maria Domenica Brun Barbantini, Concepción Cabrera de Armida (popularly known as Conchita), and Praxedes Fernandez.

Saint Brigid of Sweden, who died in 1373, was the mother of eight. (As pointed out at the beginning of this book, she is also known as Bridget, Birgitta, or Brigitta.) One daughter, Ingeborg, became a nun early in her life. Another, Cecilia, was a nun but left the convent to marry. Even in our times such a change of mind could cause a mother dismay; how much more so in her times. (Like that of other widow-saints, such as Elizabeth Ann Seton, Saint Brigid's life will be discussed at length here and in other sections of this work.)

It is related in Jorgensen's famous biography[33] that Christ told Brigid that this daughter, Cecilia, belonged to him, and that he chose that she would better grow as a married woman, so the mother should not mourn.

We find that Brigid's daughter Cecilia was twice married and widowed and at the end of her life lived as a widow in the monastery founded by her mother, Brigid, where one of Cecilia's own daughters was a nun.

Brigid had great difficulty with a son, Karl, who was caught up in the lures of sinful living and whom she eventually saw converted, partly owing to her penances for him.[34] A cook, who was serving Brigid when she was living as a pilgrim in Rome, on one occasion showed some resentment because of the strictness of his mistress. Out of spite he told her that news had come with a pilgrim from Sweden that her son Karl had been hanged while still in a state of sin. Thinking that her son was not in a good place to stand before the judgment seat of God, Brigid wept and finally cried out, "Thy will, not mine, O Lord, be done!" When it became clear that the story of his death was a lie, and the cook begged forgiveness on his deathbed, Brigid did forgive him but later had a vision of this cook sitting on a beam that was placed over the abyss of hell. But the Blessed Virgin told her that even though he was being punished for causing Brigid to grieve, he would eventually be saved.[35]

Now to turn to Brigid's problems with another daughter, Karin: How modern does this description sound of a mother's problems with an overly attractive daughter!

Karin, twenty years old, was with her mother in Rome but not allowed to go about, since she was too attractive.[36] She had to stay in her room while the others in the group went around visiting churches.

Brigid allowed her daughter to decide freely about marriage, but the young woman, in despair, thought about using a poisonous ointment to mar her face just so she could get out of the house. Her mother and confessor forbade this strategy and told her that God would protect her from shame and dishonor. She decided to go off alone to disfigure herself, but just as she started to do this, a big rock fell on her head, which injured her without killing her.

Brigid then put her daughter under the guidance of her confessor, Master Petrus. As a result of his holy advice, Karin placed herself in the hands of Saint Sebastian and then she felt brave enough to venture forth into the world outside the confines of her home. Once some bandits were about to rape her at a pilgrim inn, but God sent angels disguised as soldiers to protect her.[37]

Of the twin boys of Saint Rita we know that they were of a violent temper from early childhood. Their raging attitudes increased when their father was murdered. They caused their saintly mother much concern but died in an epidemic renouncing their plans for revenge. You will read more of this story in a later chapter.

The difficulties of raising children alone come out in a slightly different way in the case of Saint Jane de Chantal. As mentioned before, to provide her children economic advantages and avoid having them disinherited, she had to live in the immoral household of her father-in-law, who kept a mistress and the children of their illicit union.

Jane was not able to take steps toward becoming a consecrated nun until she had settled her children successfully, and this involved many problems. In the course of her struggles, one daughter died young, while another married a brother of Saint Francis de Sales and resided close to the convent Jane eventually founded.

Jane's daughter Françoise came with her to the community for a time but later married. During a period of turmoil when Françoise was uncertain about whom she should choose as a husband, Jane advised her daughter to pick a man fifteen years older than her rather than a rash, dissolute, young fool like most of the young men of that day.[38]

Françoise tended to love vanity and luxury and was naturally anxious concerning the advice offered by her saintly mother. Not one to scorn natural marital joys,

Jane recommended that Françoise be careful to make her husband as happy as possible in the "duties required of you by God."[39]

In time Françoise herself was widowed and eventually returned to her mother. In response to a letter when her daughter was still grieving the death of her husband, Jane wrote:

> Truly, your sorrow is great, and, when looked at only in terms of this earthly life, it is overwhelming. But if you can look beyond the ordinary and shifting events of life and consider the infinite blessings and consolations of eternity, you would find comfort . . . as well as joy in the assured destiny of him for whom you mourn.
>
> Oh, when will we learn to be more attentive to these truths of our faith? . . . But, imperfect as we are, we somehow transform into poison the very medicine the Great Physician prescribes for our healing . . . let us surrender ourselves lovingly to the will of our heavenly Father and cooperate with His plan to unite us intimately to Himself through suffering. If we do that, He will become all for us: our brother, son, husband, mother, our all in all. Courage! . . . I beg our Lord to help you find the rich treasure which His Goodness has hidden at the very core of the pain that comes to you from His hand.[40]

And here is some very timely advice for widows written to the same daughter a little later:

> My greatest wish is that you love like a true Christian widow, unpretentious in your dress and actions and especially reserved in your relationships, having nothing to do with vain, worldly young men. Otherwise, dear, even though I am very sure that your con-

duct is above reproach — others could question and criticize it. . . .

I know very well, darling, of course, that we can't live in the world without enjoying some of its pleasures, but take my words for it, dearest, you won't find any really lasting joys except in God, in living virtuously, raising your children well. . . . If you seek happiness elsewhere, you will experience much anguish, as I well know. . . .

I am not against the legitimate pleasure you can derive, by way of diversion, from healthy relationships with good people . . . check your inclinations and surrender them to God for His glory dwelling in you, for the respect and love you owe to the memory of your beloved husband, the preservation of your good name, and the benefit of your daughter who, undoubtedly, will model herself after you.[41]

There follows advice on how to live a Christian life in the world with morning prayer, commitment to do good and avoid evil, prayers to the Holy Spirit and the Blessed Virgin, and the like. She suggests daily Mass as much as possible, readings especially from the books of Saint Francis de Sales, and a regular examination of conscience.

Returning to the time when Jane was leaving the family for the convent, the last of her children to be provided for was a fifteen-year-old son. For a year before the break he had been lovingly informed of his good future within the extended family. Nonetheless, in a dramatic teenage gesture he threw himself over the threshold when his mother was on her way to the convent so everyone could see how "you trampled on your own child."[42]

In a letter of spiritual direction, Saint Francis de Sales urged Jane de Chantal to try to plant in the soul of her son a desire to serve God: ". . . you will have to minimize the idea of purely human glory, but do this very gradually; as he grows up, with God's help, we shall think of specific ways of doing this."[43]

And here is some advice that sounds unbearably contemporary: ". . . take care that he and his sisters sleep alone, as far as possible, or with persons whom you can trust as completely as you would yourself. I can't tell you how important this is: experience [in the confessional?] teaches me this every day."[44]

He suggests that Jane not pressure one of her daughters to be a nun. She should want to of her own accord, not to please others or because of coercion.

Saint Louise de Marillac had only one son to worry about. Even as a child, this boy was difficult. By the age of twenty-three, without a father's hand, he had become unstable and wayward.[45] He had given up the dream of becoming a priest. Eventually, however, her son married a good woman and became a father.

Like Saint Louise, Blessed Marie of the Incarnation, of the seventeenth century, had only one son. After her widowhood she kept him with the extended family while she worked long hours in the carting business of her brother-in-law. Meanwhile, contemplating her love for Christ, she longed for the convent. Finally, when her son was eleven years old, Marie's spiritual director told her to enter the convent of the Ursulines in response to the obvious prompting of the Holy Spirit in this direction.

In this context, it is helpful to remember that in those days the extended family was much more of a reality. Claude had been living with his mother in the household of his aunt and uncle since babyhood.

It was painful enough to have to separate from him to be a Sister in the same town. Much harder was it to part with him in young manhood when she left as a missionary to Canada from which, in those days, it was most unlikely she would ever return. In one of her typical letters she wrote to her son:

> Your letter brought me so profound a consolation that it is very hard for me to describe it. All this year I have been in great torment, imagining the pitfalls where you might stumble. But finally our gracious God gave me peace in the belief that his loving and fatherly goodness would never lose what had been abandoned for his love. . . . You have been abandoned by your mother and your relatives, yet hasn't this abandonment been to your advantage? When I left you before you were twelve years old, I endured terrible agonies of spirit which were known to God alone. I had to obey his divine will . . . my heart was strengthened so that I was able to overcome what had delayed my entry into religious life for ten long years. . . . I foresaw that you would be abandoned by your relatives, which caused me a thousand pains; this, linked to human weakness, made me fear your ruin.[46]

It is certainly not the teaching of the Church that widows should leave their young children to enter a vowed life. Certainly the sanctity of Marie of the Incarnation is not based on that choice. Nonetheless, it is part of her holiness that she endured the agony of that decision out of a conviction that it was God's will.

Eventually Marie's son became a holy priest, in the process being brought by his own graces to understand and accept the choice of his mother that had been so painful to him in his adolescence.

The children of Saint Elizabeth Seton were more of a consolation than a concern, at least until they were older. This first American-born saint had five children: Anna Maria, William, Richard, Catherine, and Rebecca, all very close in age, seven years separating the oldest from the youngest. Her eldest daughter, when eight years old, accompanied her on the voyage to Italy that ended in her widowhood. (You will read more of this tale in the chapter where her whole story is given.) After her husband died, she had to wait six months before seeing the youngest four children again.

Elizabeth wrote in a letter to a friend: "Once more to see my darlings seems to me more happiness than I dare to ask for — My William charged me always to make them look for him in heaven. . . ."[47]

Two of the daughters died before Elizabeth, cherished to the last moment in the arms of their beloved mother. Elizabeth worried a lot about her sons. They were good but not talented or ambitious. She had hoped one might feel called to the priesthood, but she would never press this hope unless it clearly came from God.[48]

"I have no earthly interest for them — only one point in view — their precious souls and dear Eternity," she wrote.

As is the case with so many Catholic mothers, and especially divorced or widowed, Elizabeth was terrified that once out in the world, following the termination of their formal Catholic education, her sons would fall into sin.

(You probably have noticed by now that I have been switching back and forth on the stories of the widow-saints featured in this work. One of the reasons I am doing this is to focus on different aspects of their lives that I hope will be relevant to those of you who are widows.)

I was only able to learn a little about Blessed Maria Domenica Brun Barbantini (1789-1868) of Lucca, Italy, but if her story interests you, it may be possible for you to find out more.

Blessed Maria Domenica was married at twenty-two, and her husband died six months later. She gave birth to their child, a boy, whom she raised. She also took over her husband's business and helped the needy, forming a group of women called the Pious Union of the Sisters of Charity. She actively promoted what was called Catholic Action. Blessed Maria's son died when he was eight years old. With the help of a priest she also founded the Sister Servants of the Sick of Saint Camillus in 1829.

Conchita, the holy Mexican woman, to whom I have referred often before, co-founded several orders. Nonetheless, she always thought her duties as a mother were her primary concern.[49]

She writes: "In my life as a child, my family life had so many imperfections! And in my life as a wife, how many regrets [I have]. I could neither be a daughter nor a wife. Let us see whether as a widow, I am going to seek my perfection and become a saint on carrying out the sacred duties of a mother."[50]

The widow's concern to raise her children to be holy occupied the greatest part of her time. Conchita prayed separately for each one regarding what was necessary in terms of virtues and state of life.

She felt unutterable anguish when one of her boys died while her husband was still alive, and then again, when the youngest of the eight living ones suddenly drowned in the swimming pool of the house. Another son died at age eighteen after a sickness, probably typhoid fever.[51]

Two of Conchita's children took religious vows — her son Manuel as a Jesuit missionary, entailing the terrible prospect of lifelong separation, and her daughter Concha as a contemplative Sister of the Cross. She had to watch this daughter die also, this one of tuberculosis.[52] The four surviving children became exemplary laypersons.

When the adult children were interviewed by Conchita's biographer, Philipon, they all said she was a wonderful mother. She was always pleasant, full of fun, spontaneous, loving, firm and energetic, and normal, never putting on holy affectations, visiting with guests of all kinds, and always helping the poor.[53] The only fault her children could mention was a fondness for candy.[54]

Conchita's spirituality is that of a victim soul, praying for detachment from earthly things. Yet she does not think it necessary to pretend to be so detached as to feel no pain at the gradual loss of her family.

After her last son's marriage, Conchita wrote in a manner that will endear her to many a mother-widow: "Now all is over for me. God gave me nine children. He has taken away all nine, may He be blessed! Two religious, the others dead or married, all, one after another have been snatched from my maternal heart. Their beds, including that of my husband, are now empty and here I am now alone. Yet no, not alone, I have Christ who does not die, who does not part from me, and who will never abandon me."[55]

## *Economic Problems*

Sometimes we imagine that the saints were so holy they never thought about money problems at all. I was relieved to find out that even the most sublime did have concerns. They resolved these difficulties with greater trust in God than many of us can boast of, but the problems are not so different. I think you will find the stories in this section moving in their depiction of the heroism of some widow-saints, and sometimes also funny, as in this incident from the life of Saint Brigid of Sweden.

Even though Saint Brigid, born into a family of high nobility, had chosen the poverty of a pilgrim, when living in Rome she felt bad that others of the Italian nobility would see how poorly she and her daughter really lived. Sometimes God would perform a miracle to save her vanity. Once a surprise visitor had his sight "confused" and saw rich bedspreads when they were really sleeping on straw!

For a long time Brigid lived with her daughter, her confessor, and an entourage of disciples in Rome at the palace of a cardinal who was in Avignon. Suddenly he decided to return and told them to look elsewhere for lodgings. Brigid, who was not rich, had to borrow money (which she often did) to find a place. She also did not hesitate to loan money to those in need. Fortunately for her, God on more than one occasion miraculously sent the money she needed.[56]

Saint Jane de Chantal was another widow who suffered greatly from the new economic situation she found herself in after the death of her husband. It is hard for us to get a picture of her situation, especially since legal matters in those times and circumstances were somewhat different from ours. Apparently if she had gone back to her father's house with her children after becoming a widow, she would lose all inheritance for them from their father's side. Prudence seemed to dictate moving in with her tyrannical father-in-law. Without this problem, Jane would certainly have gone back to her father's home. Even after the children were grown up, she had to return from the convent to the world to take care of accounts and disordered legal matters whenever they arose.

Even though Saint Louise de Marillac (died 1660) belonged to the upper strata of seventeenth-century Parisian society, when her husband died she had to sell their large house and move into a poorer neighborhood. However, she was delighted to have the freedom now to live more simply with one maid instead of a retinue and without obligations to attend functions at theaters and drawing rooms. So beloved was she by her rich friends, however, that they often came in their luxurious carriages to visit her and benefit from her good counsel and her prayers.[57]

At the death of her husband when Marie of the Incarnation was but nineteen, the widow found herself not only with a baby but "with debts so large she was advised that bankruptcy was her only recourse."[58] Undaunted, the capable young woman salvaged everything she could.

At first she lived in her father's house, supporting herself with fine needlework. Soon we find her also at her sister's household during the day, with grandmother taking care of the little boy. Later Marie moved into her sister's house to supervise the domestic help, to cook, tend to the sick, and take care of the workmen of her brother-in-law's carting business. Eventually she became the chief manager of her brother-in-law's business.[59] Although Marie hated the work, which included dealing with cursing longshoremen, checking invoices and merchandise, and watering all of the horses, she did it so well that no one could believe how much it made her suffer.

As described earlier, Blessed Marguerite d'Youville, our eighteenth-century Canadian saint, was left virtually bankrupt after paying off her husband's gambling debts. So that their joint property could be used to pay off business debts, she had to renounce all rights to inheritance for herself and her sons, and sell off all the valuable furniture, silverware, etc. Marguerite supported the family by means of income from a small store where she sold her needlework, cloth, and sundries. Her family helped her get merchandise on favorable terms. Townspeople were delighted to be served by so gracious and honest a businesswoman. Soon the customers discovered in the holy widow not only a source of good supplies but also an ear for their troubles.

Here are some of the specifically economic difficulties Saint Elizabeth Seton faced as a widow. (Ironically, when she was the well-to-do wife of a prosperous New

York businessman, she was a co-founder of a society for the relief of poor widows with small children.) Elizabeth's husband died virtually bankrupt when she had five small children to support. Normally the well-off relatives would have taken care of them, but these Episcopalians were so horrified by Elizabeth's reception into the Roman Catholic Church that, for the most part, they abandoned her. They also feared that members of their families might follow Elizabeth's lead and convert to Catholicism.

Her friend and mentor Antonio Filicchi, who claimed to have the "exclusive right of regal friend and Brother,"[60] tried to help Elizabeth by arranging an annual collection from her friends in various parts of the world, but most of them gradually stopped paying into this fund. Our widow-saint tried to raise money by teaching and taking in boarders, but the Protestant parents of the children were afraid their youngsters would be influenced in one way or another to join the Church.[61] As you will see from accounts later on in this book, Antonio and his brother bore most of the burden of supporting Elizabeth and her family for many years.

Here is a paragraph from a letter she wrote in 1805 that reflects her anxieties: "The so long agitated plan is given up, and in consequence I am plagued for a House, wearied with consultations about what would be best for me, etc., and certainly the painful ideas suggested by my present circumstances would weigh down my spirits if they were not supported and so fully occupied by interior consolations . . . my heart is free of all concern, redoubles its prayers, prepares for its dear Master . . . received him happy, grateful, joyful, and most truely Blessed."[62]

Saint Elizabeth Seton was happy to find a nice but inexpensive dwelling close to a Catholic church so that she could easily attend Mass on a daily basis. Consideration of both the affordability of living quarters and their proximity to a church might be important for many widows.

It is difficult for us to imagine some of the duties of a widowed mother in straitened circumstances during the 1800s. Our saint writes of preparing winter clothing for the children, "mending and turning old things to best account" and in that occupation being up until midnight or even one in the morning.[63]

Moreover, she longs to have her young boys in a good Catholic school, which she cannot afford, for they are being influenced badly by relatives and acquaintances of an anti-Catholic disposition.[64]

Elizabeth was ready for any occupation that would prevent her from having to stay with relatives and live again as a "lady." She was advised by some to run a tea or china shop. "They do not know what to do with me, but God does — and when his blessed time is come we shall know, and in the mean time he makes his poorest feeblest creature Strong."[65]

Since Elizabeth's health was poor, she was fearful of what might happen to her little ones if she died and had to leave them in the hands of her Protestant relatives.[66]

Often in the midst of her trials it is the "sweet promise of death"[67] that brings her solace.

It took quite a few years for different clergymen, impressed by her character and teaching ideas, to get her situated in Maryland, first in Baltimore, and then at Emmitsburg, where she founded the Sisters of Charity of Saint Joseph. As a consecrated woman with her own daughters to support (her sons were placed in a nearby Catholic boys' academy), she lived in great simplicity and often grinding poverty but was able to survive. The snow used to come in through the roof onto their faces at night in one of their experimental dwellings.

It will bring a smile to your lips to note that in 1818 she was warned about the city as a dangerous place for her sons to make their way in the world after graduation because of the "depravity of the young people of our cities."[68]

Eventually Elizabeth had to send her adult sons away to make their own futures. One became a seaman, another a businessman. Here she writes about the separation (caused by economic necessity) at a time when it might take many months for even a letter to get to its destination across the ocean:

> William William William is it possible the cry of my heart dont reach yours; I carry your beloved name before the tabernacle and repeat it there as my prayer, in torrents of tears which our God alone understands. [As pointed out earlier, the editors of Saint Elizabeth Seton's memoirs have evidently chosen to publish her material practically verbatim, including errors and inconsistencies in punctuation and the like.]
>
> Childish weakness fond partiality you would say half pained if you could see from your present scene the agonized heart of your Mother but its agony is not for our present separation my beloved one, it is our long eternal years which press on it beyond all expression — to lose you here a few years of so embittered a life is but the common lot, but to love as I love you and lose you forever oh unutterable anguish — a whole Eternity miserable, a whole Eternity the enemy of God, and such a God as he is to US — dreading so much our Faith is quite lost having everything to extinguish, and nothing to nourish it. . . .[69]

Praxedes Fernandez was reduced to abject poverty by her widowhood. Her husband had been a poor miner. After his death she had to move back to her mother's house. Her unmarried sister was afraid that the return of her sister and four sons would adversely affect their upper-middle-class lifestyle. Praxedes decided to allay this anxiety by accepting only room and board and doing the work of the servant, who was then dismissed as unnecessary. This Spanish holy woman also took in sewing and had to remake old garments into suitable clothing for her boys as did Elizabeth Seton. (As with other widow-saints in this work, there will be more on Praxedes Fernandez in a subsequent section.)

## *Relatives*

It is characteristic of many widows of our time to go through a period of difficulty trying to discern new directions after the death of a husband. In this chapter we will mostly describe positive experiences of help given to such widows in their process of discernment. We will begin, however, with widow-saints who found their own relations to be an obstacle to the new paths they wished to choose.

Take Blessed Angela of Foligno, for example, one of the most dramatic of Italian mystical saints. She was one of these widows whose relatives sought to block her on her spiritual journey. Perhaps a description of one of these incidents will find you more on the side of the relative than that of Angela.

Inflamed with the spectacular graces that accompanied her conversion, Blessed Angela felt impelled from within to shout out her experiences in public. A relative rebuked her for this display and told her not to return to the Basilica of Saint Francis in Assisi, which seemed to especially lead to such proclamations! You might like to know that this relative later became her disciple.

Blessed Jane (or Jeanne) de Maille, who died in 1414, lived a celibate life with her husband. Only thirty years old when her husband died, she was literally kicked out of the castle by his family because they believed she was squandering the family wealth on the poor.[70]

After the many trials Marguerite d'Youville endured as a married woman, her own family wanted to make sure the rest of the life of their beloved relative would be happy. They thought she could resume a life in the festive well-to-do society she had come from. They were disappointed to find that under the guidance of her director Marguerite was eager instead to live among the poor.[71]

The relatives of Saint Elizabeth Seton wanted the widow to continue to live like a society lady. She risked real poverty in an effort to escape from a lifestyle she found incompatible with her goals of simplicity.[72]

Elizabeth was also vilified by relatives for being the instrument whereby one of the young women on her husband's side of the family became a Roman Catholic.[73] The convert Cecilia was threatened with exile from America. The anti-Catholic relatives resolved never to speak to either of them again.

These family members became still more furious when one of the daughters who was a society belle became a fervent Catholic and then died shortly afterward around the same time as Cecilia. Even though lung disease was a family problem, they blamed Elizabeth for the early death of the young woman, since she died in Elizabeth's convent.[74]

## Help from the Church

You will no doubt be surprised that what we now think of as "grieving groups," or widow groups, already had a place in the fourteenth century. We read that when Saint Brigid of Sweden was in Rome, she was surrounded by women, some of whom were widows like herself.

Even though the women saints of the past seldom thought in precisely these terms, it is clear when reading their stories that plunging into care for the needy provided healing of their own sadness and loneliness. In the section of our book entitled "Widow Roles — The

Saints Show the Way" we will have long descriptions of widow-saints devoted to charitable works.

A form of sacrificial love for others that may be inspiring for Catholic widows today is modeled for us in a moving way by Conchita. Whereas we might find ourselves with plenty of time on our hands to be critical of the Church and its priests, this Mexican widow-saint devoted herself to prayer and penance for the most sinful members of the clergy.[75]

Under this heading, "Help from the Church," regarding ways the Church has helped some widow-saints to find their path, I will touch on these areas especially: help in discernment from friends and advisers, scriptural perspectives, and how Mass and Holy Communion helped our saints to survive and eventually to flourish.

### Discernment: Friends and Advisers

This section will familiarize you with some of the most interesting stories of spiritual direction in the annals of Church history, which may lead one to wonder whether the widow's plight leads to even more difficulties in this sometimes complicated relationship than in other friendships.

The spiritual journey of Blessed Angela of Foligno, most of which took place after she became a widow, was shared by a scribe and confessor, one Arnaldo, possibly the chaplain of the bishop of Foligno.[76] Even though Arnaldo took down her revelations in the safety of sitting in the church, there were some who thought he spent too much time with her. Accordingly, he sometimes sent a boy instead to take down the thoughts she wished to share with others.

Blessed Angela also had a dear friend in a holy man who felt called to give everything away and took a vow of absolute poverty at the same time she did.[77]

Her closest spiritual companion was a woman friend

and probably a servant: Masazuola, who lived with Angela after her widowhood.[78] This woman was a source of information for her confessor, Arnaldo, concerning mystical phenomena she observed on a daily basis. Angela revered her as a holy woman with special mystical graces in her own right. In fact, once when she asked Christ to send her friend a special grace of the same sort as her own, he told her that the grace he would give her friend would be different.[79]

However, many spiritual advisers thought Angela crazy or possessed, especially because she wanted to live so stripped of worldly goods. Members of the Franciscan Order often sided against Angela, thinking her to be a false mystic.[80] It was during a trip to Rome that she finally got papal permission to live in the kind of poverty preached in the Gospel.[81]

One locution from the Holy Spirit to Blessed Angela is of special importance concerning how much friends can help one on the journey to holiness. Angela was told that God would not have been able to give her certain graces if she were with less worthy companions.[82] This shows that we must be careful to be close to those who are themselves open to mystical graces if we are to receive as many as God might want to give us.

Saint Brigid had for help a priest-chaplain who stayed with her on her travels and in Rome. He served as her confessor and also could bring the sacraments to all those Brigid managed to bring to conversion. Besides friends on earth, Brigid also had heavenly helpers. When she was living in Rome, Saint Agnes taught her how to read Latin and speak it well enough to teach pilgrims from many lands. If she had been able to speak only in Swedish she could never have had the influence she did in Rome.

Concerning how to discern whether locutions and visions were coming from Christ or from the Devil, the

Blessed Virgin told Brigid: "Fear not that what you now see and hear has come from an evil spirit. For as the sun brings light and warmth, which the dark shadow does not bring, so the Holy Ghost, when it enters into the heart of a man, brings two things: the warmth of love and the light of faith. You feel these two now, and they do not go with the devil."

Outside of the friendship of Saint Francis and Saint Clare of Assisi, it would be hard to find an example of a woman saint where so much depended on the advice of a male saint as in the case of Saint Jane de Chantal and her mentor Saint Francis de Sales. Before their auspicious meeting some years after Jane became a widow, each had a vision from God of the physical form of the other with a conviction from the Holy Spirit that this was the person who would help most with the fulfilling of Christ's will.

So closely did God wish them to be joined in a "bond of perfection" that the holy priest could write Jane in all simplicity: "I know you have complete confidence in my affection; I have no doubt about this and delight in the thought. I want you to know and to believe that I have an intense and very special desire to serve you with all my strength. . . . I believe it is from God. . . . Make the most of my affection and of all that God has given me for the service of your soul. . . ."[83]

Here is a letter of advice that specifically refers to the blessings and pitfalls of widowhood: ". . . those who do not like their widowhood are widows in appearance only, for their hearts are still married. . . . Praise God who has given you this precious, holy love [of Christ]; help it to grow more and more each day, and your own consolation will increase proportionately. . . . Avoid anxiety and worries, for nothing so impedes our progress toward perfection. Place your heart in our Lord's wounds gently, and not by force. . . ."[84]

Francis de Sales gave the widow Jane, during the many years she was forced to remain in the world, advice that could apply to the problems of many a widow. He urged her not to look into the future with anxiety but to serve God within the family.[85]

Often widows with children can be tempted to idealize the contemplative life. De Sales wrote to his married sister: "Let us all belong to God . . . in the midst of so much busyness brought on by the diversity of worldly things. Where could we give better witness to our fidelity than in the midst of things going wrong? Ah, dearest daughter, my sister, solitude has its assaults, the world its busyness; in either place we must be courageous, since in either place divine help is available to those who trust in God and who humbly and gently beg for His fatherly assistance."[86]

De Sales was the inspiration for the Visitation community of women he would help Jane form. This religious order would embody his own ideals for the spiritual life. Not only did he visit frequently to give sublime conferences but also took part in the most seemingly mundane decisions of the group of devout women under his direction. I especially love the understanding of our feminine nature that Saint Francis exhibited when watching them working on the habit. He insisted that they make it a little more attractive. He said that he wanted them to be holy but not hideous!

One of the most important spiritual friendships in terms of the apostolate came from the collaboration of Saint Louise de Marillac and Saint Vincent de Paul. It is noteworthy that Saint Louise began by conceiving a dislike for the well-known preacher who seemed to her to be too cold and austere. Indeed, even as her director, Saint Vincent, in spite of his holiness, treated her with a severity that shocks us to read about.[87] He wanted to ensure that she would live for God alone by advising her always to seek God rather than his own counsel. Yet he wept openly after her death when talking about her with one of the communities they had founded together.[88] It is interesting that he tried to moderate her scrupulosity by discouraging her from making up little rules of life and fasting too much.

These two saints spent many decades collaborating on ministry to the poor in a spirit of heroic sacrifice, as will be described more fully in another chapter. "God alone knows. . . ," he once wrote to her, "what He has done for me in giving you to me. In heaven you will know."[89]

Blessed Marguerite d'Youville received much of her formation as a helper of the poor of the city of Montreal from her spiritual director, Father Dulescoat.[90] He saw in this widow the gifts of heart and mind necessary to develop a full-scale approach to the miseries of the needy. In a short biography of his saintly mother, Marguerite's priest son, Charles, wrote this about her relationship to this director: "She was not one of those persons who importune their confessors from morning till night, piling up a hundred conferences without drawing any profit from them . . . eager to change confessors, wanting to be directed by everyone they meet. . . ."[91]

After this fine priest's death, another Sulpician, Father Normant, became Marguerite's director. He was as interested in the growth of her own soul, especially through devotion to the Sacred Heart and to the Holy Family, as in the charity to the poor that overflowed from her love of God. It was this same director who eventually would encourage Marguerite to take the poor into her own home and to found an order of women that would be called the Grey Sisters. More about these apostolates in the chapter about widow-saints ministering to the needy.[92] (See "Widow Roles — The Saints Show the Way.")

The support and advice of friends, as a help to a

ST. ANGELA'S PARISH LIBRARY
146 8TH STREET
PACIFIC GROVE, CA 93950

widow, has rarely been more tenderly portrayed than in the friendship extended to Elizabeth Seton by the Filicchi family of Italy. Unable to leave Italy for six months after the death of her husband, Elizabeth and her eight-year-old daughter lived with these Italian family friends and business partners of her husband.

In a letter back home Elizabeth wrote that her daughter said, "O Mamma, how many friends God has provided for us in this strange land, for they are our friends before they know us."[93]

She continued: "[At Antonio Filicchi's house] we received more than Friendship, — the most tender affection could not bestow more, and to crown all his goodness to me he has taken my passage [on a ship] who sails direct for New York . . . and accompanies us himself, as business and a wish to be acquainted with our country has long made the voyage necessary to him and now the desire of restoring his 'dear sister' to her children and those she loves best, decides him to leave his dear little wife and children — he says this is due to all my dear [husband's] love and Friendship for him."[94]

Once in the United States, Antonio sought to give Elizabeth every help toward her conversion, which took place soon after her return. Antonio, whose letters and very occasional visits she treasured, became a brother to her.[95] She described him as "the friend, protector, and consoler of the widow and the fatherless," who would receive a great reward in heaven.[96]

More about this spiritual friendship can be found elsewhere in this book.

It was shortly after her husband's death that Conchita encountered the holy priest with whom she would co-found several religious orders. An interior sense led her to visit a particular church for confession. She opened to this priest her whole soul, especially about her sense of the delight of suffering with Christ on the Cross, and her belief that she was called to promote a spiritual path called the Works of the Cross. This priest, Father Felix Rougier, who had experienced the same calling himself, became her spiritual director. His cause for beatification is being considered together with that of Conchita.

This friendship was itself nailed to the Cross, for Father Felix's superiors thought that he should not associate with such a woman mystic. He was exiled for ten years to Europe, where he served in lowly capacities.[97]

Conchita's biographer remarks that Father Felix was not a dreamer but a mature, realistic person with a rock-like strength. He was a great help to her in the founding of several orders, the two exchanging advice and, most of all, encouragement in the path of holiness.[98]

All the authorities in the Church that were asked to discern whether Conchita was on the right spiritual path supported her in her prayer life and in her goals for the founding of the Works of the Cross.[99]

A few words about the life of Mother María Luisa Josefa of the Blessed Sacrament (died 1937), foundress of the Discalced Carmelite Sisters of the Third Order. Mother María was born in 1866 into a family of fourteen children in the province of Jalisco, Mexico. She was married to a doctor twice her age. Together they helped the sick, aged, and poor. She was widowed at the age of twenty-nine. Twice in twenty-six years she tried to enter a convent. The archbishop told her that God did not want her there, but instead she should return to the hospital she had founded with her husband. At the hospital, young women joined her in the work.

Finally, in 1921, the archbishop approved of a new religious congregation — the Carmelite Sisters of the Sacred heart. By now María Luisa was fifty-five years old. She would now be called María Luisa Josefa of the Blessed Sacrament. This order still stresses contemplation. In 1927, persecuted by the anticlerical Mexican government, Mother Luisita, as she was called, traveled to Los Angeles, California. Eight Carmelite houses were founded as a result, with the novitiate in Alhambra, now part of the Los Angeles metropolis. She is most often quoted as saying, "If we do our best, God will do the rest." After two years in the U.S., she returned to Guadalajara. Her cause for canonization has been introduced.

### Scriptural Perspectives

It is helpful to a widow to read the many passages in Scripture admonishing the community to help poor widows. We also become intrigued about the references in the New Testament to widows who themselves exercised ministry in the early Church. Scripture may be especially uplifting because of the very positive appreciation of the widow in the Bible, an affirmation that contrasts with the somewhat negative societal image in many present-day cultures.

We find in Scripture various passages about forlorn widows, heroic widows, and widows free for service to others in the early Church.

Let us look at the famous story of Ruth, the Moabite woman who married a son of Elimelech and Naomi after this couple had migrated and settled in Moab to escape famine.

After the death of her husband and two sons, Naomi journeyed back toward Judah, since the famine had ended. Both her daughters-in-law loved her and didn't want to live without her. Naomi thought it would be better for the young widows to seek husbands of their own culture, since she said she was too old to remarry to provide husbands for them, even if they wanted to wait until such sons would be old enough for marriage! One daughter-in-law, Orpah, left; but Ruth clung to Naomi apparently not only because she loved her mother-in-law so much but also because she preferred the religion of the people of God. We read the famous passage, often quoted in wedding ceremonies: ". . . for where you go I will go, and where you lodge, I will lodge; your people shall be my people, and your God my God" (Ruth 1:16). Rereading these lines now as a widow, I wonder if the way Ruth clung to her mother-in-law is indicative of how abandoned a widow could feel and how much family can mean in such circumstances.

Such desperation is reflected in Naomi on her return to Bethlehem, asking her people to call her not Naomi (which means pleasant) but Mara (which means bitter), for coming back with neither husband nor sons (see Ruth 1:20-21). In the well-known story of how Ruth finds a husband in Boaz, a wealthy landowner, by gleaning in his fields, we see that she was impoverished by her widowhood.

Before marrying her, Boaz protects her by charging the young men in the field not to molest her (Ruth: 2:9). From these lines we realize that a young widow without father or brothers would find herself in danger, risking sexual assault to find food in an alien land.

Boaz compliments Ruth for seeking shelter under the wings of the Lord God of Israel (Ruth 2:12). It is Naomi who suggests that Ruth offer herself as a wife to Boaz by visiting him when he has eaten well and is taking his rest. He is pleased that she has chosen him instead of one of the younger men and that she is reputed to be "a woman of worth" (Ruth 3:11).

In a formal ceremony of those times, Boaz offered to buy the land of Naomi's former husband, thereby also gaining the right to take Ruth as his own. Only when the community validated this right did he take Ruth as his wife. In due time she bore him a son and in this way the widow Naomi was also blessed with next of kin who could support her in her old age. Naomi became the wet nurse of the baby. He was called Obed and became the father of Jesse, who was the father of David (Ruth 4:13-17), of whom Jesus was considered a direct descendant.

Can we find a hint in the story of the two widows, Naomi and Ruth, about the need even in our times for older widows and well-to-do self-controlled older men to help widows so that they may not become prey to the sexual desires of sometimes irresponsible younger men?

One of the most beloved of heroic widows was Judith, described in the Apocrypha.[100] Judith was a pious woman who lived at home as a widow for three years and four months fasting, devoted to God (Judith 8:4-8). She delivered the Hebrews from the Assyrian tyrant Holofernes by enticing him; then, risking her life, she assassinated him (Judith 13:1-8). Many wanted to marry this famous, beautiful woman, but Judith remained a widow all the days of her life, dying at the age of one hundred five. She was revered as a teacher of the elders of the city.

It is doubtful if many widows will be in a position to save the lives of their people by pretending to seduce a powerful enemy of their countrymen. Some insights, however, that we can take away from the story of Judith is that a devout widow without children to care for, engaging in spiritual warfare through prayer and fasting, is in a powerful position to respond to God's call, whatever it might be, such as going to jail in connection with pro-life protests, or becoming a missionary in a dangerous country.

Although Scripture does not give us much detail about the daily life of Mary, Jesus' mother, in her life as a widow, many of us take comfort in thinking about her sorrows and identifying ourselves with her losses. The last chapter of this book will be about Mary as a widow.

A widow story in Acts 9:36-42, which delights me, is the one about the raising of Tabitha (Dorcas) from the dead, seemingly because she was so useful to the community they couldn't do without her!

Now there was at Joppa a disciple named Tabitha, which means Dorcas or Gazelle. She was full of good works and acts of charity. In those days she fell sick and died; and when they had washed her, they laid her in an upper room. Since Lydda was near Joppa, the disciples, hearing that Peter was there, sent two men to him entreating him, "Please come to us without delay." So Peter rose and went with them. And when he had come, they took him to the upper room. All the widows stood beside him weeping, and showing coats and garments which Dorcas made while she was with them. But Peter put them all outside and knelt down and prayed; then turning to the body he said, "Tabitha, rise." And she opened her eyes, and when she saw Peter she sat up. And he gave her his hand and lifted her up. Then calling the saints and widows he presented her alive. And it became known throughout Joppa, and many believed in the Lord.

I think this story shows that widows were quite active among the disciples; moreover, that they were close to each other, and also that they were much valued by the male disciples.

The only full-scale treatment of the status of widows in biblical times that I found was by Bonnie Bowman Thurston, a Scripture scholar and professor, called *The Widows: A Women's Ministry in the Early Church.*[101] The rest of this section will be devoted to highlights of this scholar's research that you can ponder to draw your own conclusions.

From the earliest times of Israel's history there was support given to widows. The Hebrew word for widow, *almanah*, is derived from the word *alem* meaning unable to speak, related to a word meaning to be in pain. The sense is not that widows became mute, but that they were not spoken for.[102]

In the Old Testament, for a husband to die before a still-fertile wife was considered to be a sign of retribution for sins. The widow shared a sense of being disgraced. This is reflected in the story of Naomi, Ruth's mother-in-law, who calls herself afflicted and bitter (Ruth 1:20-21).

A widow had various options. Her birth family could pay her purchase price to her husband's heirs, or she could remain in his family in a lowly status. She could remarry, but it was considered better to wait to marry a brother of her husband to ensure the male line.

A widow could not inherit.[103] That is why she was to be the beneficiary of charity. In this way God protected her through the services of the community (Psalm 68:5; Proverbs 15:25).

Men were commended who helped widows (Job 29:13). Those who mistreated widows were to be condemned in the day of judgment (Job 31:16, 28).

The figure of the New Testament's Anna, who was early widowed and spent her time in the temple praying and waiting for the coming of the Messiah, is a paradigm for Christian widows. The mention of her in the Gospel of Luke signifies that there was a precedent in the Jewish world for consecrated elderly women.[104]

"And there was a prophetess, Anna, the daughter of Phanuel, of the tribe of Asher; she was of a great age, having lived with her husband seven years from her virginity, and as a widow till she was eighty-four. She did not depart from the temple, worshiping with fasting and prayer night and day. And coming up at that very hour she gave thanks to God, and spoke of him to all who were looking for the redemption of Jerusalem" (Luke 2:36-38).

It is surmised that she may have fasted more than the customary Mondays and Thursdays and clearly spent more than the usual amount of time in prayer than was expected. As a prophetess she would be accepted as a woman inspired by God to make God's will known to others.

Some say that Jesus was especially sensitive to widows because he knew his mother would be one. The climax of this compassion could be seen in his giving of his mother at the crucifixion into the hands of one of his disciples, thought to be John.

Among biblical passages where Jesus specifically refers to widows are the following:

Mark 12:38-40 describes some leaders who devour widows' houses. The passage about the widow's mite (Mark 12:41-44; Luke 21:1-4) may indicate that widows wore a special dress, since Jesus seems to have pointed her out without knowing her personally. The widow's gift becomes a symbol of total self-giving and trust in Divine Providence.

The widow of Nain (Luke 7:11-17) is represented as being overcome with grief because it is her only son who has died, which means she lacks all legal protection. The famous passage in Luke 18:1-8, about the widow who wears out the judge by nagging him, is making use of the symbol of the widow whom God especially cares for to show how we should pray with confidence.

Thurston believes that the widow in the teachings of Jesus asserts a "new system of values breaking into the world." The widow's status is not sad but important in Christianity. The widow becomes a shining example of how God "has put down the mighty from their thrones, and exalted those of low degree" (Luke 1:52).[105]

Mention of widows in Acts gives us images both of the care of widows and also of an emerging group of widows in ministry. Some passages in Scripture and accounts of the early Church give the impression of an ecclesial order of widows, but the actual status of the widows is a matter of scholarly dispute.

In Acts 6:1-7 there is mention of a controversy over the status of widows of different origins: Hebrews and Hellenists. The newly appointed deacons were to see to this provision. Thurston explains that in the *Jewish* practice of the time a widow who had less than a week's supply of food at home could apply for food collected from alms at the temple. Such widows were cut off when they became *Christians.*[106]

Mention of widows in Acts 9 is sometimes interpreted as implying the existence of an "order" of widows selected from among the larger group for ministry.[107]

In 1 Timothy 5:3-16 we find some of the most puzzling and some of the most challenging teachings. I will present this passage as separate paragraphs, basically sentence by sentence, for greater ease in study:

> Honor widows who are real widows.
>
> If a widow has children or grandchildren, let them first learn their religious duty to their own family and make some return to their parents; for this is acceptable in the sight of God.
>
> She who is a real widow, and is left all alone, has set her hope on God and continues in supplications and prayers night and day; whereas she who is self-indulgent is dead even while she lives.
>
> Command this, so that they may be without reproach.
>
> If any one does not provide for his relatives, and especially for his own family, he has disowned the faith and is worse than an unbeliever.
>
> Let a widow be enrolled if she is not less than sixty years of age, having been the wife of one husband; and she must be well attested for her good deeds, as one who has brought up children, shown hospitality, washed the feet of the saints, relieved the afflicted, and devoted herself to doing good in every way.

But refuse to enroll younger widows; for when they grow wanton against Christ they desire to marry, and so they incur condemnation for having violated their first pledge.

Besides that, they learn to be idlers, gadding about from house to house, and not only idlers but gossips and busybodies, saying what they should not.

So I would have younger widows marry, bear children, rule their households, and give the enemy no occasion to revile us.

For some have already strayed after Satan.

If any believing woman has relatives who are widows, let her assist them; let the church not be burdened, so that it may assist those who are real widows.

I must admit that certain ideas in this famous passage never hit me until becoming a widow myself — such as gadding about and gossiping. Having fallen into this pattern for a while, I can understand what a temptation such behavior can be for the rootless, relatively homeless widow who no longer has the settled lifestyle of a married woman. Deprived of the usual regular family members to converse with, we can easily develop a gossipy tongue as we go about from house to house seeking warmth and comfort.

On a more formal note, here are some of the comments on this passage that Bonnie Bowman Thurston found important to ponder.

The concept of "enrollment" implies that there was a pledge to lifetime widowhood for the sake of Christ. The idea that a widow would be unfaithful who reneged on this pledge can be seen as a forerunner of women's religious orders. Thurston indicates that a special status for widows makes it possible for some Christian women to be independent of the family structure.

The widows, whom Scripture describes as authentic widows, are to have the virtues of good Christian women: teaching children, offering hospitality, and practicing humility while serving the less fortunate.

The first duty of widows is prayer and intercession with a view to contemplation.[108] Thurston links this choice of a greater life of prayer to the aging process, which tends to limit active service. Freedom from household duties gives widows more time for devotion. She alludes to the viewpoint of some scholars who think that the weekday community worship of the early Church was frequented especially by widows *just as now*. Having no one to depend upon, the widow is more likely to hope in God, a hope nourished by prayer.

In Titus 2:4-5 we are told that the older women are apt teachers of younger ones in feminine virtues of kindness, chastity, and submissiveness.

The book we have been quoting from, *The Widows*, also includes chapters about the status of widows in the apostolic period. A few quotations may be helpful.

Ignatius of Antioch gave these instructions: "Let not the widows be wanderers about, nor fond of dainties, nor gadders from house to house; but let them be like Judith, noted for her seriousness; and like Anna, eminent for her sobriety."[109]

Polycarp, bishop of Smyrna, was enjoined by Ignatius to be the guardian of widows. In his own writings Polycarp describes the widow as "an altar of God."[110] Because widows are altars of God they are to avoid all evil, including love of money. They are to intercede for all, in the spirit not of Martha but of Mary. The image of the widow as an altar of God includes the concept of the burnt offering, obeying God and sacrificing of herself by giving service to the community and also avoiding sinful or scandalous behavior.[111] More prosaically, some Fathers of the Church consider, instead, that the phrase "altar of God" simply referred to the fact that widows received their sustenance from the assembly of worship around the altar.[112]

Praying in front of jails where Christians were being detained or tortured was one of the activities widows were known for during apostolic times. The pagans described these widows as old hags,[113] perhaps because Christian widows were not well dressed.

One theologian of early Church days mentions that a chaste widow is especially to be honored in a way different from virgins because "it is easy not to crave after that which you know not, and to turn away from what you have never had to regret."[114] The same theologian warns against drink and curiosity. Instead the widow should be occupied with counsel and comfort.[115]

The famous *Didache* of the third-century Church describes widows as in the likeness of the altar.[116] It states that no widow under fifty years of age may join the "order" of widows lest she later marry and cause scandal or deplete the Church's resources when she is marriageable.

The bishop was responsible for assuring support for widows and orphans and was to make certain the benefactors were honorable in their intentions. Widows are not to teach the faith in the way that Jesus appointed the apostles to do or baptize, but instead to pray, do good works (including making clothes, working at wool, and visiting), lay hands on the sick, and fast. They are not to visit homes without permission of the hierarchy.[117] Widows were exhorted to be meek and quiet and gentle, not chatterers.[118]

### The Mass and Holy Communion

It would be impossible to quote all the passages from the lives of the widow-saints that refer to the solace they experienced from participating in Holy Mass and receiving the Body and Blood of the Lord. I will include only a few notations here.

Right after the death of her husband in Italy, before becoming a Catholic herself, Elizabeth Seton found every way to go to church for the liturgy. Here she could shed tears unnoticed, the others being so absorbed in their own prayers.[119] Seeing the Blessed Sacrament passing under her window in procession, she was moved to think about the Catholic conviction concerning the Real Presence that she, as an Episcopalian, did not yet fully believe: "I face the full loneliness and sadness of my case I cannot stop the tears at the thought my God how happy would I be even so far away from all so dear, if I could find you in the church as they do. . . ."[120]

Elizabeth Seton was very impressed by the fact that Catholics could go to daily Mass.[121] When she became a Catholic herself, at her First Communion, she wrote to Amabilia Filicchi: "God is mine and I am his . . . a triumph of joy and gladness that the deliverer was come, and my defence and shield and strength and Salvation made mine for this World and the next . . . now then all the excesses of my heart found their play and it danced with more fervor . . . perhaps almost with as much as the royal prophets before his Ark . . . truly I feel all the powers of my soul held fast by him who came with so much Majesty to take possession of this little poor Kingdom."[122]

During a time of fear about her future, with no clear path and many monetary worries, Elizabeth wrote in a letter: "I never was so happy — in the brightest years of my life, never experienced an enjoyment to be compared with a moments Blessedness at communion."[123]

Toward the end of her life, when her own health was failing, she wrote that she was "living in the very Sanctuary of the divine presence going to sleep at night [waking] in the morning almost before the blessed [altar] for we have but a partition between my little room and our chapel."[124] (There will be more on Saint Elizabeth Seton later on in this volume.)

Conchita, the holy grandmother of Mexico, wrote in her diary that, in her widowhood, "I sense His presence, above all on receiving Communion, flooding me with His light, with His rays and purifying me . . . he impels me, by the acceptance of sacrifice, to crucify myself, to desire suffering, martyrdom, to give my blood every day for the salvation of souls."[125]

# Widow Roles — The Saints Show the Way

This chapter will provide you with stories about a number of widow-saints highlighting especially the choices they made in Church work after the death of their husbands. I have selected certain saints as key witnesses for each role.

It is my hope that this reading will help you see how typical it is for widows to go through struggles in finding where they belong. In some cases it may happen, as I pray, that the story of a particular vocation within the Church will fan the flames of some hope of your own. The categories of callings include (in no particular order): helper of the needy, intercessor, penitent, pilgrim, prophetess, martyr, contemplative, nun, Sister, and foundress.

## *Helping the Needy*

### Key Witnesses: Saint Elizabeth of Hungary and Praxedes Fernandez

***The Witness of Saint Elizabeth of Hungary*** ❀ One of the most famous young widow-saints was Elizabeth of Hungary. Information about her life is taken from a book about her by Nesta do Robeck.[1]

The life of this saint, who lived from 1207 to 1231, could be considered a wonderful — but, to some, odd — "riches to rags" story. As an infant of a royal family, Elizabeth was betrothed to Louis of Thuringia. At four years of age she was taken in procession to Thuringia to be prepared for her future life as a queen.

But the little girl was not at all of the princess type. Serious and prayerful, she was ridiculed by the adults in the court. Happily, the one person who totally understood her was her future spouse, for he was the same way. Together the young people dreamed of the great deeds they could do for Christ when they grew up.

Elizabeth and Louis were married when he was twenty-one and she was fourteen. They loved each other deeply and spent many hours in prayer together. During the night when her husband was asleep, Elizabeth would kneel in prayer, holding his hand in hers. When he left on knightly excursions, she would follow in his retinue as long as possible, weeping and praying for his safe return.

They had three children, one of whom became Blessed Gertrude. Elizabeth herself was to be the first Germanic member of the Franciscan Third Order. She loved to help the poor. During famines she gave away the store of grain at the castle to the needy; moreover, she built a hospital for the ill, tending them with her own hands. Each day she fed nine hundred people who came to her gate starving. Elizabeth of Hungary is considered to be the patroness of bakers!

Also, to the horror of the royal family, she sold the jewels that were heirlooms to finance her works of mercy.

When Louis died in a Crusade, Elizabeth wailed for days. "Dead! Henceforth all earthly joys and honors are dead to me!" she exclaimed.[2]

The death of Louis enabled his relatives to banish the hated pious princess, who disgusted them with her religious ways. They feared her fanatical religious acts would impoverish them also. Indeed she once sold property that was not her own out of ignorance. Later Louis' family would ask her forgiveness and bring her back to continue her works of mercy with their approval.

But immediately following her widowhood, Elizabeth knew poverty, homelessness, and persecution. All these trials she endured because of the simultaneous ecstatic mystical experiences she was enjoying. It was with gaiety that Elizabeth donned beggar's rags as she continued to serve the poor, with herself and her children now also members of the class of the poorest.

The first night our widow-saint left the castle she spent the night in a pigsty. Two faithful companions came with her. Delighted to finally be able to live like Saint Francis, Elizabeth rejoiced in her new freedom. Her biographer describes her as being like a willow growing by the riverside. When a flood comes, the willow bends. Undamaged, it straightens out after the flood.

Is that the secret of fruitful widowhood? To bend like a willow with adversity until we can stand strong again in the Lord?

Finally the ex-princess was given a financial settlement from Louis' family. She established a hospital in Marburg, where she lived in small quarters. She was free now to nurse and care for the ill without worrying about her relatives' fears. In the sick she always saw the Lord.

Elizabeth was obliged by her relatives to give up her children. Hermann and Sophie were sent off to be raised for political roles. But Gertrude was allowed to go to the Premonstratensian monastery, as requested by her dying father.

At the time of parting, Elizabeth confided them to the Lord to do with as he pleased. Far from feeling rejected, they were all proud to be the children of such a saintly mother.

The source of Saint Elizabeth's strength was her contemplative prayer and frequent reception of the Eucharist. Often she was seen with a shining face after receiving Communion. She described seeing the heavens open, and Jesus consoling her for all the sufferings of her life, making her entirely his.

At the age of twenty-four Saint Elizabeth died peacefully, surrounded by loved ones, including a beggar child she had nursed from scurvy. At her death the singing of multitudes of birds could be heard just as at the death of Saint Francis.

**The Witness of Praxedes Fernandez** ❀ A perfect example of a contemporary widow-saint who devoted herself to helping her own children and all needy persons she could minister to is the holy woman being considered for canonization: Praxedes Fernandez.

Information for this section is taken from the book by Father Martin-Maria Olive, O.P., *Praxedes: Wife, Mother, Widow and Lay Dominican.*[3]

First a thumbnail sketch of the life of Praxedes before she became a widow.

As a child, born in 1886 to a well-to-do but hardworking family in the mining district of Asturias, Spain, Praxedes was unusually pious. She was devoted to Christ and his Church and to the needs of the poor. One of those attractive and competent girls who are appreciated by everyone in the family, Praxedes was described by her siblings as lovable and obedient. By the age of eleven, she became her mother's right arm in housekeeping, running the store, and taking care of the garden.

For a short while Praxedes went to a Dominican school. She was a good student and also showed much interest in spirituality. She was described by the nuns as intelligent, pious, calm, tranquil, irreproachable in virtue, and always generously giving of her time to other students.

Praxedes practiced constant prayer in the midst of the duties of family life that were sufficiently plentiful to require her to interrupt her education.

Sought after by a number of young men as a bride, Praxedes was, nonetheless, reluctant to marry. She finally accepted the proposal of Gabriel Fernandez, a simple laborer who worked in the mines. She was fond of him because of his basic goodness, even though he tended to be irascible.

Mother of many children, coming quickly one after another, Praxedes enjoyed her hidden life as the wife of a worker. She used to say, "I wish I could be like those violets hidden in the weeds, but still giving off such a pleasing aroma."[4] She had learned from the story of Saint Zita, a servant-saint, how to pray continually while doing menial tasks.

But Praxedes's husband did not share his wife's spiritual fervor. He began objecting to how much time she spent in church. Once when she had been meditating on the passion, he slapped her in the face. Praxedes never complained about his harsh treatment, but a neighbor went to his mother about it. The mother-in-law of Praxedes was outraged, for she admired her son's wife very much. The mother-in-law had a heart-to-heart talk with her son, and he never hurt Praxedes in this way again.

Sorrow came into the personal life of Praxedes with the death of her beloved father and then a freak train accident that killed her husband. Afraid that her spouse might have died in sin, she spent much time praying for his salvation and was eventually reassured that he was safe with the Lord.

At the death of her husband, Praxedes was left penniless with her four children. Praxedes decided to move in with her mother and an unmarried sister. In exchange for room and board, she was happy to cook, clean, garden, wash, and serve at the table. In fact, in response to an objection her sister made that the large addition of five people to the family would increase expenses, Praxedes insisted on doing all the work previously done by the servant. To provide some money for clothing for her children, as well as education, she took in sewing for others.

Visitors to the house were horrified to see Praxedes working so slavishly, since the family actually did have enough money to make do without such sacrifices. The necessity mostly stemmed from the attitude of Praxedes's sister, an unmarried schoolteacher who disliked having children in the home. So spiteful was this sister that she kept under lock and key the best food for herself, forcing Praxedes and her sons to dine separately on inferior food. Outraged friends of the family could do nothing to change these practices, since Praxedes herself never complained. She thought of these humiliations solely in supernatural terms, as crosses to offer to the Lord.

In spite of her many duties in the house, Praxedes always made time for Mass. She taught others that "the time it takes to assist at Mass, far from being an impediment, serves to help you do them [chores] even better."[5]

This Spanish holy woman spent many hours in teaching her own children how to pray during Mass, about the passion of Jesus, the Blessed Virgin, sin, the wiles of the Devil, and the dangers of bad companions. Her greatest desire was that one of her sons would be called by God to become a priest. After her death, one son, Enrique, took final vows as a Dominican friar.

So efficient was Praxedes at her own housework that she always had time to visit the sick, collect clothing and food for the poor, and also pray in depth for two hours every day. She was especially devoted to Jesus in the tabernacle, once seeing the Lord in the Host surrounded by a glorious light. Praxedes was much inspired by reading the lives of the saints, especially Saint Teresa of Ávila.

Then came the Communist revolution in Spain, and Praxedes found herself living in a Communist-dominated parish. Because of the violence, the bishop sent the parish priest away. Yet the same communistic people who refused to have anything to do with the Church loved Praxedes for her charity to one and all. She would help those who supported the Church as well as those who hated it. "If all Catholics were like Praxedes," they would say, "then we would believe in religions."[6]

Tragedy struck again when one of her sons, age fifteen, was killed in a train accident. The mother understood that she was to suffer as Christ suffered.[7] As Saint Teresa of Ávila taught, those whom God loves he takes through trials: the more the love, the greater the trials.

During the revolutionary times, Praxedes began to attend three Masses a day: one to prepare for Communion, the second for actually receiving Communion, and the third for giving thanks. At these Masses she was given many graces, especially the assurance of the salvation of her deceased husband and son.

When all the priests were massacred or exiled, Praxedes was the one to go from house to house baptizing babies, comforting the sick, and preparing the dying for their final journey.

As the violence increased, Praxedes dedicated her life to penance for her country. "All this is happening because there is no prayer life and there are no sacrifices in the lives of the people," she used to say.[8] Praxedes knew that voluntary suffering, accepted and joined to that of Jesus, contributes to the salvation of the world.

Penances included fasting, putting beans into her shoes to make walking uncomfortable, and flagellation (done in secret in the chicken coop).

Praxedes's works of mercy increased as the poverty

and suffering caused by the war increased. She was called "the Mother of the poor."[9] In many ways she reminds me of the late Mother Teresa of Calcutta.

Besides corporal works of mercy, her very presence was a grace to others. Maintaining her calm amidst bombings, she assured those hiding in her home that there was nothing to fear. Only the loss of souls was important. She refused to let anyone pass harsh judgment on Communists, instead praying for their conversion.[10]

During this time she became a Third Order Dominican, taking the name Catalina in honor of Saint Catherine of Siena.

In 1934, the whole family moved into a larger house in another town where there was still sacramental life. Now she could receive Holy Communion often. The prophetic gift became strong in the spirit of Praxedes, who predicted another war. In 1935, she offered herself as a victim of reparation for the future war. But Praxedes also predicted that the Blessed Virgin would be with us and that the Sacred Heart would eventually triumph.[11]

In 1936, while nursing the sick during a typhoid epidemic, Praxedes contracted the disease herself. So peacefully did she die that those around her couldn't believe she was dead. The humble violet was finally buried in the garden of her beloved.

The mother of Praxedes believed her daughter to have been a saint.[12] Even her mean sister, during inquiries about the holiness of Praxedes, confessed that her sister was exemplary.

# Intercession, Penitence, Pilgrimage

## Key Witness: Blessed Angela of Foligno

### The Witness of Blessed Angela of Foligno ✤
Blessed Angela of Foligno (1248-1309) was one of the

most fascinating penitential widow-saints in the history of the Church. I will outline her life story and then quote extensively from biographical and autobiographical writings. My chief source of information can be found in *Angela of Foligno: Complete Works.*[13]

Angela was born in Foligno, twenty miles from Assisi, in the middle of the thirteenth century. She married young and had seven children. She describes herself as being a sinful woman, and implies that these were sins of adultery during her married life, though some scholars think she may have been less advanced in a life of sin than she herself hints.

In her late thirties, Angela made a pilgrimage to Assisi and, having a sudden dramatic conversion, became a Third Order Franciscan. Within a short time all of her family died. She decided to live in poverty, penance, and care of the needy, free from the bondage of the expected social life for women of her class. Soon the holy mystic was surrounded by loving disciples, both women and men.

I think of Angela as a spiritual version of the heroines of Italian opera, for she was so theatrical in the expression of her religious emotions that even her followers didn't know what to do with her. Her visions left her with so much fire, fervor, and joy that when she heard anyone speak of God she would cry out aloud in public.

At first, after her conversion on the road to Assisi, Angela experienced tremendous consolations; but later she went through periods of demonic affliction and hideous temptations, some to sins she had never even imagined in her youth. Blessed Angela's account of her life of prayer is contained in *The Book of Divine Consolation*, which was one of the most beloved and popular writings of a woman mystic during many of the centuries following her death. It is noteworthy that much of her writing was dictated to her scribe and confessor, Franciscan Brother Arnaldo.

From the introduction to her writings, by Paul Lachance, O.F.M., I share with you certain facts and realities about the life of Blessed Angela that may be of interest to you:

• The wooden statue of Angela containing her relics and depicted on the cover of the *Complete Works* indicates that she was seen as a short and round woman.

• Facts about her life are somewhat scanty, but scholars agree more or less that she came from a well-to-do family and that she was orphaned on her father's side very young. It does not appear that she studied in any formal way, but it is clear that she was quick, intelligent, and open to learning.

• She seems to have married when she was twenty years old, and to have had several sons. The whole immediate family, with the exception of Angela, is considered to have died around 1288. Biographical writers think that her own writings about sins that are important to confess is a portrait of her own life before her conversion. Among these are to be mentioned such vanities as hair-dressing, perfume, luxurious clothing, excessively fancy foods, longing for possessions, foolish conversation, detraction, anger and pride, as well as engaging in "illicit caresses and seductive behavior."[14]

Angela's conversion started in 1285 when she began to fear damnation and, weeping bitterly, went to confession but was too ashamed to tell the priest every sin so that she was receiving Holy Communion sacrilegiously.

In prayer, she begged Saint Francis from heaven to find her a worthy confessor, and she found a good one who absolved her of all her sins. For five years after that, Angela tried to liberate herself from sin. She gave her property to the poor and adopted the habit of the Third Order of Saint Francis.

On pilgrimage to Assisi, she begged for the grace to feel Christ's presence in her soul and to observe the rule perfectly. It was at a wayside shrine that she had an extraordinary grace in an experience of the Trinity. On the same pilgrimage, sensing Christ's presence in an intense way, she became afraid of losing this loving tender feeling, and she threw herself on the floor of the Basilica of Saint Francis shouting in an unintelligible way.[15] Her confessor, Arnaldo, was ashamed of her and told her not to come back.

Angela experienced for several years great joy and peace from the graces of the pilgrimage. When Arnaldo was assigned to Foligno, he questioned her about her behavior, on the theory that it was caused by demons, but gradually became so impressed that he became her scribe.

After this relatively happy period of divine revelations and ecstatic visions, Angela began to experience, in 1294, despair and abandonment as well as intimacy and union. She felt both chosen and damned. She had to struggle with terrible demonic temptations.

The last thirteen years of her life were spent primarily in being a spiritual mother to a small community that gathered around her. Her teachings are assembled in the book called *Instructions*. On her deathbed she said that Christ had come to tell her that he would come for her himself.

We now turn to specific quotations from the words of Blessed Angela dictated to Brother Arnaldo beginning with the "outline" of the way of penance. It should be noted that her penitential path predated her widowhood but was intensified after she was free "to leave the world," even more.

I find Angela's way of penance to be difficult, even though inspiring, reading. The idea of penance has always been to me repugnant in the extreme, since daily life seemed difficult enough without adding anything. However, at times I get inklings that I am being called to such a path, if only to take an attitude of consciously accepting both the little and the terrible sufferings of life *as a penance*, to be offered to Christ generously in reparation for my sins.

For those readers who feel clearly called to a life of penance, or think they might be so called in the future, here are some excerpts from this mighty work of Blessed Angela (Chapter I of *The Memorial*: The First Twenty Steps of the Blessed Angela in the Way of Penance and Spiritual Perfection):[16]

Each of these steps takes time. It is indeed very pitiful and truly heartbreaking that the soul is so sluggish and moves so painfully and ponderously toward God. It takes such tiny steps at a time.[17]

The first step is the awareness of one's sinfulness . . . in it the soul weeps bitterly. The second step is the confession of sins. The soul still experiences shame and bitterness. There is not yet the feeling of love, only grief. She [Blessed Angela] told me how she had often received communion in a state of sin because she had been too ashamed to make a full confession . . . the third step is the penance the soul performs in satisfaction to God for its sins, and it is still grief-stricken.

The fourth step is the growing awareness of divine mercy which is granted the soul . . . [awareness of] forgiveness and [that divine mercy] snatched it from hell. The soul begins to be enlightened, and then it weeps and grieves even more than before, and undertakes even sharper penance.

The fifth step is knowledge of self when the soul sees nothing but defects in itself. The sixth step consists of realizing the depths of one's sins — seeing how God and all creatures have been offended. . . .

[From this point on, Brother Arnaldo is quoting Blessed Angela verbatim.]

I was given to pray with a great fire of love invoking all the saints and the Blessed Virgin. . . . As a result, it did seem to me that all creatures had mercy on me, and all the saints.

In the seventh step I was given the grace of beginning to look at the cross on which I saw Christ who had died for us. What I saw was still without savor, but it did cause me much grief. . . .

In the eighth step . . . I felt that I myself had crucified Christ . . . set me so afire that, standing near the cross, I stripped myself of all my clothing and offered my whole self to him. Although very fearful, I promised him then to maintain perpetual chastity . . . on the one hand, I feared to make this promise, but on the other hand, the fire of which I spoke drew it out of me, and I could not do otherwise.

In the ninth step, it was given to me to seek the way of the cross. . . . This would entail forgiving all who had offended me, stripping myself of everything worldly, of all attachments to men and women, of my friends and relatives, and everyone else, and, likewise, of my possessions and even my very self. Then I would be free to give my heart to Christ . . . and to walk along the thorny path . . . the path of tribulations.

[After this Blessed Angela reports that she gave away her best clothing, fine foods, and fancy headdress. Her husband was still alive and she was slandered for this behavior. Soon after this the whole family died and she felt that now] . . . my heart would always be within God's heart, and God's heart always within mine.[18]

In the tenth step, [Christ] appeared to me many times, both while I was asleep and awake, crucified on the cross. He told me that I should look at his wounds. [He showed her how each wound was incurred for her sins.] . . . I wept much, shedding such hot tears that they burned my flesh. I had to apply water to cool it.

In the eleventh step . . . I was moved to perform even harsher penance. [The translator mentions that the type of penances performed during this period of Church history included such practices as praying with arms outstretched for long periods, wearing iron chains and hair shirts, flagellating oneself, and fasting on bread and water for long periods of time.][19]

In the twelfth step . . . [she decided to live as much as possible in total poverty in spite of fear of hunger, cold, and nakedness, begging, even though this could be dangerous; she resolved to trust that even if she died of such privations, she would be happy in God].

In the thirteenth step . . . [she entered into the] sorrow over the passion suffered by the mother of Christ and Saint John.[20] [She came to love the heart of Christ.]

In the fourteenth step . . . He called me to place my mouth to the wound in his side. It seemed to me that I saw and drank the blood, which was freshly flowing from his side. [This blood was to cleanse her. She felt great joy at this blessing but at the same time sadness about the passion and a desire to suffer as he did.]

In the fifteenth step . . . [she understands what John experienced of sorrow at the crucifixion (see John 19:26-27); this gave her a greater resolve to get rid of her possessions no matter what her mentors said to dissuade her[21]; still she felt no relief, only bitter sorrow for her sins].

In the sixteenth step . . . [she was able to understand the meaning of each line of the Our Father, and she began to know the divine sweetness in meditating on the goodness of God].

In the seventeenth step . . . [she sees that it was Mary who obtained for her the grace of conversion; she receives consolation in dreams and visions and a grace of continual divine sweetness].

[By] the eighteenth step . . . [she felt such joy in prayer that she forgot to eat and wished she did not need to eat; but she saw that it was a temptation not to eat].[22] The fire in my heart became so intense that if I heard anyone speak about God I would scream. [People thought her possessed. Her woman companion had to hide paintings of the passion to stop her from running a fever when contemplating them.]

[During] the nineteenth step . . . [she went into a trance from contemplating the divinity and humanity of Christ].

Here the text is broken while Brother Arnaldo relates how he came to know Blessed Angela and start writing down an account of her experiences. Of special note in the narratives that follow are these:[23]

• The promise of the Holy Spirit to be with her forever as her spouse, more beloved than anyone in the Valley of Spoleto because of her total surrender to Christ: "I am much more prepared to give than you are to receive."[24]

• That it is important to see that penance is accompanied by tremendous joyful graces.

• On receiving graces of great love from the Holy Spirit in the Church of Saint Francis in Assisi, she feels pain when Jesus withdraws from her and shouts out, "Love still unknown, why do you leave me? Why? Why? Why?"

• On the road home Jesus said, "Your whole life, your eating, drinking, sleeping, and all that you do are pleasing to me."[25]

For eight days Blessed Angela had such a sense of intimacy with God that it is described by her scribe as mystical betrothal. The account of this is summarized in the chapter toward the end of our book explicitly about Christ the Second Bridegroom.

The account given of the intimate experiences of Blessed Angela includes a salutary analogy that we can all apply to ourselves even if we are not as penitential or mystical as Angela. "We have no excuse for not receiving Christ's love. We should come to him humbly as a sick person goes to the doctor and, revealing our illness, open ourselves to the doctor's remedy."[26]

Christ also explained that he gives special graces to those who return to him from a life of sin because of his joy in their return: graces he does not grant to others who were virgins and had not sinned.[27]

## *Prophetesses*

The word prophetess in this section is used in its widest meaning, as referring to those who come against the evils of the world in the name of God. For example, we read that the widow Blessed Jane de Maille (1332-1414) got a king in France to liberate all the prisoners in Tours.[28] To my mind this links her closely with prophetic women of the Old Testament times such as Esther or Judith.

### Key Witness: Saint Brigid of Sweden

*The Witness of Saint Brigid of Sweden* ❀ Saint Brigid of Sweden (1323-1373) lived so many different roles that she could easily be considered the prototype for any of our categories, as you will see from my outline of her history. I have put her among the prophetess widow-saints because that is the part of her story that most singles her out in Church history.

The information about Brigid is taken from *Saint Bridget of Sweden*, Johannes Jorgensen's famous biography.

The night Brigid was born, the seventh child, the priest saw a vision of the Blessed Virgin Mary, who said to him that Brigid's "wondrous voice shall be heard all over the world."[29]

Brigid's parents were very pious and of high rank in Swedish society. If you read Jorgensen's biography of this saint, it is easy to see that God used Brigid's knowledge of the life of the court so that she might play a prophetic role in these influential circles. Her mother loved God above all.

Even as a young girl, Brigid received special visions concerning the meaning of Christ's passion for the salvation of sinners. Brigid was beautiful, pious, and learned. It is noteworthy that it was she who suggested that the Scriptures be translated into Swedish.

Although Brigid wanted to be a nun, she willingly agreed to marry Prince Ulf at the age of fourteen. She loved him dearly. Brigid was happily married for twenty-eight years and, after two years of agreed-upon abstinence, bore four sons and four daughters. She especially enjoyed giving her children religious instruction. The holy woman also brought them with her to personally tend the sick among them in the hospital.

Brigid was a Third Order Franciscan. In penitential style, she wore a hair shirt under her fashionable courtly clothing and exercised a prophetic ministry by challenging society people to live according to the Gospel. It was during this time that Christ appeared to Brigid and told her to form a double monastery of nuns and monks at Vadstena: "Thou shalt not only be counted my bride, but also a nun and mother in Vadstena." The nuns were to be ascetical and contemplative and the priests to continue in active apostolic work as well as serving the nuns.

On pilgrimages with her husband, Brigid herself felt a great yearning to become a contemplative nun; but Christ told her that even when she became a widow he wanted her to remain in court, in order to convert her relatives and friends. During the period before the death of her husband, Ulf, there were reported innumerable miracles of healing at her touch as well as conversion of sinners from whom she cast out devils. Brigid was constantly ordered by God to stand up against murder, looting, rape, and unnatural sexual sins that were rampant in Sweden in those times.[30] Long afterward, in Rome and Naples, she would also prophesy against abortion and slavery.

In the realm of Church politics, Brigid, when sent by God to Rome, would be told by the Lord how to try to reconcile the Avignon pope with the emperor. She lived in Rome for many years, doing intercessory prayer in the pilgrim churches, and would eventually see Charles IV accompany Pope Urban back to Rome from France.

I want to concentrate on the part of Brigid's life as a widow when she was having many visions and being told often by saints how to conduct her life.

In one vision Saint Agnes showed her how important it was that she use her scholarship to defend the truth through Scripture rather than stay home and spin.[31]

In another vision the Blessed Virgin told Brigid that she must write to a cardinal to tell him about how the Church was being ruined by the sexual sins and greediness of many ecclesiastics, with the assurance that God would grace those who repaired such damage.[32]

Brigid had a priest among her entourage in Rome. Often he had less knowledge about theology and languages than she did, and so he would send penitents whose language he did not understand to Brigid for discernment.[33]

At one point the Swedish saint was told by Christ to

leave Rome and visit a monastery infamous for moral abuses. She spoke for Jesus to the abbot, accusing him because of his womanizing, being a father to children of his own instead of being a father to the poor.[34]

She would write to sinners about social justice. Christ told her to advise them that whereas then self-will prevailed over conscience, in the day of judgment self-will would be silent and their own consciences would witness against them. If people with secret sins came to visit, she would sometimes cover her nose with her hand to indicate that the stench of sin was upsetting her![35]

At one point Brigid became well known in Rome for her prophecies against the evils of the Church. The common people, who were living in fear of poverty and the plague, decided it was the Scandinavian princess who was the source of all evil. They gathered in the square of the cardinal's palace, where the cardinal was protecting her, and, holding flaming torches, yelled that the witch should leave and the house be burned down. The priest barred the door, the cook was terrified, the women wept; but Brigid was found as usual in her oratory asking Christ what to do, since her activities were endangering the whole pilgrim group around her. Christ told her she must stay, and little harm was done.[36]

The archbishop of Naples once assembled all the leaders and doctors of theology to hear Brigid of Sweden proclaim God's Word. She knew Latin well enough to make the speech.[37] It was attested in the canonization process that Saint Agnes herself taught Brigid this necessary language to be able to converse with the highest men of the Church, including the Holy Father, especially to be able to share what the Blessed Virgin told her in visions.[38]

On pilgrimage to the Holy Land, Brigid received many revelations from the Virgin Mary about the Nativity, the Immaculate Conception, and the Assumption.[39] Her visions of the mysteries of the passion have greatly influenced Catholic art and music. The famous revelations about the sufferings of Christ in his passion are still being distributed for devotional purposes today.

The widow-saint also prophesied that a time would come when there would be Church unity, with one flock and one shepherd, one faith, and one clear knowledge of God.

There is not room in this account to go into the fascinating details of Brigid's dealings with the Swedish court and with others of the noble classes as she tried through prophetic warnings to disentangle politics and sin in personal and social affairs. Readers are referred to Jorgensen's great biography.

# Contemplatives

All the saints were contemplative in the sense of spending hours in intimate prayer of union with Christ. Under this category I have chosen two widow-saints, with active lives outside the cloister, who nonetheless were gifted with unusually powerful mystical graces that have had a great influence on others in the Church.

### Key Witnesses: Blessed Marie of the Incarnation and Conchita

### *The Witness of Blessed Marie of the Incarnation*
❀ Much of the information for these pages comes from *Marie of the Incarnation: Selected Writings.*[40]

Marie Guyart was born into a middle-class family of bakers in Tours, France, in the year 1599. At the early age of seven, she was much influenced by a mystical dream in which she saw the heavens open and Jesus come toward her. She was on fire with love for him and opened her arms to embrace him. He was in the form of a child himself. He took Marie in his arms and kissed her, asking if she would be his. She said yes.[41]

Even though Marie was an unusually pious young woman, her parents thought that her very practical nature suited her better for marriage, and she accepted their judgment. She was happily married to one Claude Martin, a merchant. By the age of eighteen, Marie was the mother of a son. Less than a year later, her husband died.

With her fine business mind, Marie saved her husband's business and also administered the affairs of the relatives, into whose house she eventually moved. It is awesome to discover that her most mystical experiences of Christ (including the Sacred Heart of Jesus), the Eucharist, and the Trinity took place while working on the docks among rough stevedores and watering the horses!

It was in the midst of such work, for instance, that Marie, then only twenty-one, was caught up in one of the most pivotal of the mystical experiences given to her by the Lord: "My inner eyes were opened and all the faults, sins, and imperfections that I had committed since my birth were shown to me in the most vivid detail. At the same moment I saw myself immersed in the blood of the Son of God, shed because of the sins which had been shown to me; and further realizing that it was for my salvation that this Precious Blood had been shed."[42] She goes on: "I came home changed into another person — and so powerfully changed that I did not even recognize myself. My ignorance, which had led me to think that I was perfect, that my actions were all innocent, and that I was quite a fine person, was now unmasked and I acknowledged that all my righteousness was, in fact, only sinfulness."[43]

This vision brought with it an immediate and profound conversion, characterized by a new humility and a burning love. It led Marie to a lifelong missionary zeal, motivated by the desire that none of that precious blood of redemption would go to waste but must be shared by everyone in the whole world.[44]

Many mystical illuminations followed this initial conversion, especially involving a passionate devotion to the Eucharist and to the Trinity. Marie said: "I was united to him who revealed to me the divine mysteries by which I lived, and my soul was satisfied. Filled with this food I went forth to the duties he had assigned me without ever leaving him. Then I returned to him with a redoubling of love which prompted me to seek my food in the pastures of this divine Shepherd who was constantly renewing his life and spirit in me."[45]

She added: "I found my heart beating so strangely that I was completely powerless. Had it burst open I would have found consolation in death, united to him whom I could conceive and imagine only as love. Besides all this, my heart was constantly drawn to his goodness so that he would give me his spirit, for I could conceive nothing as being good or beautiful or desirable except possessing the spirit of Jesus Christ. . . . All the powers of the soul yearn and hunger only to be in Jesus . . . following him in this life and his spirit."[46]

Making a vow of perpetual chastity during this grace-filled time helped strengthen her.[47] By the age of twenty-seven Marie was brought into the graces that have been called the mystical marriage. Some descriptions of this experience are given in the chapter about Christ as the Second Bridegroom.

Although Marie loved her son with the greatest tenderness, she also felt an ever-growing desire to enter the religious life. When her son seemed old enough to be entrusted to her extended family, Marie became an Ursuline teaching Sister.

The choice of an active rather than a purely contemplative order might surprise anyone reading about the unusually mystical experiences of Marie. The editor of her writings, Sister Irene Mahoney, explains this decision as resulting from her burning desire for the salvation of souls that was part of the teaching charism of the Ursulines.

Although Marie, at first, was ecstatic about finally taking the vows of a consecrated woman in the convent, soon she entered into a period of frightening darkness. Sister Irene surmises that this time of trial for Marie may not only have been of supernatural causation, a classical dark night of the soul, but might also have been related to the change from an active life in the world to living among novices young enough to be her daughters in the convent. There everyone was subject to the rather conformist, sometimes petty, rules. So terrible also were her fears for her son, who did everything to try to get her back, that she feared she was losing her mind.[48] Perhaps the hated activities in the world were actually a balance for this richly endowed womanly nature?

Marie's depressive state was relieved by a mystical dream in which she saw a land of great natural beauty, full of forests and mountains shrouded in mist. The picture she had seen became a reality when she journeyed to Canada for her Ursulines to help Jesuit missionaries in their ministry to the natives of Canada and also to the French settlers.

In Canada Marie would experience terrible disappointment as she watched some of the French merchants corrupting the Indians with alcohol, thereby undermining their formation as Catholics by the Jesuit missionaries and the Sisters. She also became dreadfully melancholic from trying to deal with the conflicts within her own community, blaming them all on herself. What carried her through was the strength of her faith in Christ even in darkness and also her tremendous love for the primitive native children on whom she lavished tenderness for both body and soul.

As in the case of many mystics whose writings are available, it does not seem good to me to quote extensively. To benefit the most from your sisters, the widow-saints, it is necessary to immerse yourselves in their writings when these are available so that you can "live" with them over a long period. I hope that what I have excerpted will be sufficient to inspire you to obtain the entire volume of Marie's writings (please refer to the Bibliography).

Blessed Marie died in her seventies in her Canadian monastery, longing for the total union with her Second Bridegroom in eternity, of which her mystical experiences were such a foretaste.

**The Witness of Conchita** ❦ As in the case of several other prototypes, Conchita (Concepción Cabrera de Armida) — a holy Mexican widow-grandmother, whose cause is being considered by Rome for canonization — also could be described under the category of foundress. I have chosen to narrate the largest part of her story under the title of contemplative. The reason is that I think it is her way of being a mystic in the world that will have the greatest appeal for widows who — however ardently called to a life of prayer — will, like Conchita, never live in a convent.

Let me briefly outline the life of this extraordinary woman, who died in 1937, and then focus specifically on the contemplative aspects of her call after becoming a widow. The source of information is primarily the only large book about her life presently in English, *Conchita: A Mother's Spiritual Diary*.[49]

Conchita, as she was called by all her relatives and friends, was born in 1862 in San Luis Potosí, Mexico. She was an unusually beautiful, lively young girl of the ranchero class, spending her youth horseback-riding, playing the piano, singing, and generally having a good time. Her youth was carefree insofar as education was concerned because the Catholic schools had been closed as part of government persecution of the Church.

Conchita's family was most devout. Her mother bore twelve children and was regarded as a holy woman. Conchita's father presided over the daily Rosary with the family and all the farm workers.

So delightful was our heroine that she counted twenty-two suitors before she decided on the one who seemed to love Christ the most. On her wedding day she asked of her spouse, as was the custom, for two wishes: that no matter how many children they had, her husband would let her go to daily Mass, and that he would never be jealous! Hidden away beneath the merry exterior, Conchita was a true mystic, especially devoted to the Eucharist and to penance for the sins of the world.

Very happily married, Conchita and Pancho had nine children. During the time before she was suddenly widowed, Conchita spent much time in prayer, especially making intercession for priests.

After the death of her husband, when Conchita still had to care for small children, she took over the administration of family matters; but also gradually, with the help of a holy priest, she laid the foundation for several orders devoted to what she called the Works of the Cross. These apostolates include the Sisters of the Cross, the Missionaries of the Holy Spirit, and associations of laypeople. The Holy Spirit instructed the foundress not to become a member herself of the contemplative order of Sisters but to remain in the world as a woman consecrated interiorly to Christ.

It is touching to read that in the process of her beatification, still going on, her children and grandchildren were not so much impressed by her holiness in prayer but by her perfection as a loving mother.

There are more than a hundred volumes in Spanish of her writings,[50] so there are many who think that when she is canonized she will also be added to the names of Saints Catherine of Siena and Teresa of Ávila as a doctor of the Church.

From childhood Conchita was called to contemplation:

> While riding about the countryside with my father and my sister, Clara, I spent hours reflecting on how I could manage to live in a mountain cave all by myself, far from everyone, giving myself up to penance and prayer whenever the spirit moved me. I was delighted at the thought and pondered it in my heart . . . I would ride along meditating very slowly, word for word, prayers to our Blessed Sacrament or to the Blessed Virgin . . . my childish heart found ineffable delight in all this. Up to the time of my marriage, I thought that everybody did penance and said prayers and when they did so they did not let anyone else know.
>
> I was happy, so happy when I could receive [the Eucharist]. It is an absolute necessity of my life. How often, on returning from a dance or from the theater, I received Communion the next day . . . at night I would think first about the Eucharist, then about my fiancé.[51]

When still a young girl, obliged to go to dances and the theater, Conchita felt drawn ever more into a life of prayer: "At the heart of this ocean of vanities and festivals, I felt within my soul a burning desire to learn how to pray. . . . I kept myself as much as I could in God's presence. This was enough [for me] to begin seeing a great light shed on the nothingness of worldly things, on the vanity of existence, on the beauty of God. . . . Christ drew me to himself, absorbed me, enchanted me."[52]

Once married she continued a life of constant prayer and penance and was gradually drawn into the prayer of quiet.[53] She also received many locutions that she wrote down. She felt that in spite of her husband's great goodness, marriage was not totally fulfilling[54] and drew closer and closer to Christ. He told her that her mission would be to save souls.[55] The opportunity came at the farm of a relative where she was staying. She brought together women of the town, numbering sixty, and began to teach them about the spiritual life.

She began to thirst for the salvation of souls, and finally got her director's permission to engrave the initials of the holy name of Jesus, IHS (actually the abbreviation of the Greek word for Jesus), on her bosom![56] She wanted to feel like a branded animal, belonging totally to Jesus. She felt spiritually wed to him.

After that she longed to sacrifice all for Christ. She felt elevated into union with him.[57] Pain became joy to her. She considered union with Christ on the Cross deeper than what we think of as love, which often retains elements of egocentricity.[58]

"It is only in My crucified Heart," she was told by Christ, "that the ineffable sweetness of My Heart can be tasted. Seen from the outside, the Cross is bitter and harsh, but as soon as tasted, penetrating and savoring it, there is no greater pleasure. Therein is the repose of the soul, the soul inebriated by love, therein its delights, its life."[59]

She also began to have visions of the Holy Spirit as a luminous dove. Often she wrote about being enraptured by the immensity of God, and of a great thirst for union with him.[60] She was given revelations about the eternal generation of the Son from the Father and the nature of the Trinity itself.

After her husband's death, when Conchita still had to raise her children, she wrote in her diary: "A powerful grace impels me to undertake, in my new state of life, a new way of perfection, of sacrifice, of solitude, of hidden life. . . . I understand that the Lord wants to purify me that I may be more His."[61]

She hoped that as a widow-mother she would become the saint she couldn't become before. Devoting herself wholeheartedly to her life as a mother, she also gave herself to prayer, feeling God carrying her through all the difficulties of daily life.

It was at the age of forty that Conchita experienced the most important grace of her life, called the mystical incarnation, in which Christ joined her in complete union with his sufferings.[62] In the next chapter, "Jesus: The Second Bridegroom," you will find quotations from Conchita's diary concerning this peak moment of exalted unification.

Conchita's biographer considers that the grace of this moment of becoming completely one with Christ on his Altar of Sacrifice for the salvation of souls was the key synthetic moment in the life of her soul, when all that had gone before was taken up in a new way to usher in a new phase of interior and apostolic works for the Church. Especially she was to be in spiritual union with priests.

Let me tell you at this point a little more about Conchita as a foundress. Even before becoming a widow, during her many visions of the Cross, Conchita saw interiorly a procession of nuns bearing a great red cross. This was the first intimation that she would found an order of Sisters of the Cross. According to her, the Lord also announced that there would be a congregation of men.[63]

The founding of the Missionaries of the Holy Spirit, an order of priests dedicated, among many sacramental works, to offering their own sufferings for other priests, was difficult, full of frustrations and delays. During this time nine volumes of her own life, based on her spiritual diary, were examined by the Vatican. She was summoned to go to Rome herself for a personal interview with Pope

Pius X and with the Congregation for Religious. The Holy Father gave her a special blessing and told her that he had approved all the Works of the Cross,[64] asking her to pray for him. During her interview with the monsignor from the congregation she begged that she herself might remain in a hidden life in the world and not live in any of the religious orders.

The approvals were granted eighteen years after her first visions and locutions concerning these foundations. Addressing Jesus, she wrote: "What pains, sufferings, penances, disappointments! What blood, prayers, calumnies, feelings of envy, persecutions, tears all this has cost. But it all is as nothing when I think that it was for purifying Your Works for Your greater glory."[65]

The last twenty years of her life saw Conchita's children grown up and her own life more and more one of solitude. Her external works diminished and her prayer life became more one of abandonment and immolation with an apparent remoteness of God, similar to that of Jesus on the Cross.[66]

About this period she wrote: "I am in the most complete solitude of soul, but it is God's will and God, for me, is only there where His will is found. I do not understand anything any more. I am in chaos. This need to express my soul, my desires, my impressions, even on paper, all this has disappeared. I tend to keep secret my impressions, my tastes and even my sufferings and tears. I want to hide everything in Jesus. All is for Him alone. . . . On the earth, all is shadow, vanity and lies. The real, the true, what is of value, what endures, what is, is in heaven. The earth with all its things, all of them, are but a lever to raise oneself to Him . . . if I consult my heart, I discover its affections. They have passed. Its desires, the most ardent ones, its excessive yearnings for such and such a thing, have passed. . . . I ardently desired to be a nun, now that is all the same to me: to be or not to be, to die here or there. . . . I have only one desire: that in me the divine will be done."[67]

The last part of Conchita's life was given over to experiencing Christ crucified in her own heart in a darkness of faith. In the last part of her life, "she shared in the feelings of the Crucified, abandoned by His Father." For her, her beloved Jesus had wholly disappeared. "It is as if we had never known each other," she said again and again to her innermost self.[68] Her life ended with three years of terrible physical suffering to which she added corporal penances. When Conchita died, it seemed as if her face had become the countenance of the crucified Jesus.[69]

## Sisters and Nuns

Because of the great desire of religious orders to have their foundresses canonized, there is much less information than one would suspect about widow-saints who were simple nuns and not foundresses. Of these, the most famous is Saint Rita.

**The Witness of Saint Rita of Cascia** ❀ Most of the information for this section is taken from a book by Jo Lemoine, *Rita: Saint of the Impossible*.[70]

Rita was born in 1381 in Umbria, Italy, to an older devout couple, Amata and Antonio Lotti, who had been praying for twelve years for a baby. During her pregnancy, Amata heard voices from heaven announcing that the baby would be a girl and that she should be named Rita, in honor of Saint Marguerita.

The charming story of Saint Rita of Cascia's childhood has many images prophetic of her later choices, such as this one. Once her mother tried to buy some ribbons to set off the beauty of the little girl's hair for the feast of Corpus Christi. But Rita ran away and refused them. Later asked about this incident, she replied, "Jesus will love me just as much without the ribbons. He knows that I love him so much."[71] Rita was strong, and as her parents grew feebler, she was eager to help them with the heavy work.

Growing in faith, Rita had a desire to devote herself to contemplation of Jesus on the Cross and to unite herself to him in prayer. She made herself a little area in the house for her prayers, especially meditating on the passion of Christ.[72] Impressed by the life of Saint Francis of Assisi, she longed to become a consecrated woman.

Rita's parents wanted to keep their only child nearby, and secure in the future, after their death. For these reasons they were eager to find her a strong and reliable husband. They agreed to a marriage with a handsome but quarrelsome young man, Paul de Ferdinand, who had seen and chosen Rita for his bride.[73] Although reputed for his bravery, Paul had a mean streak. He also tended to drink — which could have been part of the reason for his abusive nature — and was known to seek the company of immoral women. Rita objected to this marriage because of her dedication to the Lord, but her parents would not listen to her entreaties and prayers.[74]

The marriage from the beginning was unhappy. Rita's husband began to come home later and later at night after fights with other men during bouts of drinking. Rita stayed up to offer her husband late dinners. Paul responded with temper tantrums, throwing things around the house.

The women of the neighborhood were amazed that Rita never spoke ill of Paul, even though she was visibly battered. They nicknamed her "the woman without a grudge."[75]

On the positive side, Paul was a generous man when he was in a good mood and even helped the poor at such times. Rita was determined to help her husband to reform by means of turning the other cheek, praying for him, and doing penance for the salvation of his soul, especially by fasting.

Gradually the man began to change, impressed by the goodness of his wife and also because she was expecting a child. The child turned out to be twin boys.

Indeed, Paul was changed by his fatherhood, but the violent streak in him evidently was inherited by his twin sons, who grew to be little tigers.

When the boys were in their teens, Paul was killed by an old enemy in an ambush. A friend told the boys' mother, Rita, that her husband forgave his assassin as he lay dying. But the sons, influenced by a pervasive culture of vengeance and their own fiery tempers, vowed to find their father's murderer.

Terribly upset by the unchristian attitudes of her sons, Saint Rita prayed, "Lord, rather than allow them to carry out this horrible plan [of revenge], which is growing in them as they grow in years, take them out of this world!"[76] In fact they both died of an epidemic in spite of all the cures Rita tried to employ to save them. At the last moment they forgave their father's killer.

Now a widow and also the mother of dead sons, Rita was grieved further by her failure to be received in Saint Mary Magdalene, the monastery she wished to enter. Even though her virtue and piety were well-known and admired, it was the practice in those days to admit only young girls to religious orders.

Undaunted, Rita tried again, but was once more refused. Her third attempt ended in failure.[77] Convinced that God absolutely did want her in this particular monastery, Rita increased her prayer. Meanwhile the forty-year-old widow stripped herself of her belongings so as to be ready to enter at a moment's notice.

The manner in which God chose to convince the mother superior and the Sisters was totally miraculous. One night Rita heard a voice calling her name. A man who resembled pictures of John the Baptist was at the door. He led her out to a high mountain in the dark. There she met Saint Augustine and Saint Nicholas of Tolentino. She seems to have gone into a trance. She was discovered by the Sisters the next morning inside the closed and barred gates of the monastery of Saint Mary Magdalene in the chapel seated in one of the stalls of the nuns.[78]

The mother superior was furious when she realized it was Rita, the widow she had three times refused. The Sisters as well as the superior finally had to see the hand of God in so miraculous an occurrence.

It was easy for the holy widow to accept poverty, chastity, and obedience. What was difficult for Rita — just as in the case, for instance, of Marie of the Incarnation — was to be among so many younger women. The Devil was inflicting temptations on her to despair, to pride, and impurity even though she had never had these difficulties as a woman in the world.[79] Saint Rita met these afflictions with a spirit of patience, penance, and charity. She always wore the most tattered clothing and ate the least appetizing foods. She practiced flagellation and wore a hair shirt of thorns.

On the day of Rita's profession after her novitiate, the middle-aged nun had a most significant dream. Christ appeared to her holding up an immense ladder reaching into heaven. When she awoke she decided that she would need to climb the spiritual ladder to holiness step by step.

In the Augustinian rule of that time a cloistered Sister could still help the poor of the city. Saint Rita loved to wait on the steps of the monastery for the sick and poor so that she could minister to them. In this way she became quite well known to the townspeople of Cascia.

One of the first recorded miracles attributed to God's grace working through the widow-saint concerned an old, barren twig of deadwood. The superior insisted that Rita drag buckets of water each day to make this utterly dry twig grow. This was to be a test of her obedience. To the amazement of Sisters in the convent, who doubted the older woman's holiness, after many days the twig began to turn green. Eventually delicious grapes grew on the vine that sprouted from the twig.

One day during her time of meditation on the Cross, she was inspired to make Stations in her cell. Uniting herself to the various stages of Jesus' passion, she would often faint after scourging herself for the sake of the souls of the dead, for sinners, and for benefactors of the monastery.[80]

At the age of sixty, Rita was praying before a fresco of the crucifixion when she was moved by the Holy Spirit to beg Jesus to let one of the thorns in his crown bruise her forehead as well. "Suddenly a thorn of plaster, one that made up the crown in the fresco, began to break loose. It fell and lodged itself in the forehead of the prostrate sister," and from the wound flowed a dark pus with a disgusting smell.[81]

Some of the Sisters reacted by holding their noses when Rita came near. Others stayed out of her way. Soon the smell was so noxious that it was necessary to keep Rita alone in her cell, except during the recitation of the common prayers when she was made to stay at the back of the chapel.

The saintly mystic enjoyed a respite from this wound when she prayed to be able to go on a pilgrimage to Rome for a Holy Year during which special blessings could be obtained. The wound, which reappeared when she returned from Rome, caused her constant pain.[82]

We are told of a delightful scene that took place early on during the pilgrimage. Having been given but a small amount of money for expenses, some of the Sisters began to worry if it would be enough to take care of their needs. Crossing a bridge, Rita threw her coins into the river to show what it meant to trust in Divine Providence.[83]

During the pilgrimage Saint Rita got to see the spear that had pierced Christ's side, and also to see many people from all lands and hear their tales about the evils taking place in their countries. These experiences inspired in this widow-saint an even more fervent desire to do penance for all the world.

Since Rita was isolated from the rest of the nuns because of the stench of her wound, messages were carried to her about needs of those in the town, and often graces were given as she would pray and make sacrifices for the various intentions. Sometimes there were spectacular results attributed to Rita's intercession, such as perfect health for a bedridden little girl in constant pain after her mother went to the convent asking for special prayers for her daughter.[84]

By the end of her life Rita was living on the Holy Eucharist alone. A relative came to visit and was asked by the dying nun to get her a rose and then later a fig from the garden of her old village house. As it was in the dead of winter, everyone was amazed when the cousin came back with both of these "miraculous" items.[85]

When Saint Rita was seventy-six, she was lying one evening in her cell when she was suddenly surrounded by a bright light in which she saw the silhouettes of Jesus and Mary standing at the door of her cell. Jesus promised to take her to heaven in three days. At the moment of her death the bells pealed of themselves as on a feast day. The terrible stench from the wound on Rita's forehead vanished, while the wound itself shone like a star.[86]

After her death many came to see for the last time the body of the woman they already revered as a saint. A relative with a paralyzed arm was instantly healed. So also was an ex-carpenter who wished he could make the coffin but whose disabled hand prevented him from doing so. Healed immediately, he was able to make the required wooden coffin. Soon the line of pilgrims increased as the people begged the intercession of Saint Rita, called the Saint of the Impossible. Throughout the centuries, miracles have taken place in Cascia. It was in 1628, after the institution of a scrupulous investigation of claims regarding "so-called saints," that Saint Rita, following two years of study, was beatified; she was canonized in 1900 after even more careful research. Her body has remained intact.

People come from all over the world with petitions to Saint Rita, whose body now lies in state in a basilica. This humble widow's little house is now a chapel. Near these places are orphanages for girls and boys — so Saint Rita is still a mother even from heaven.

One of the books I read about Saint Rita (the one by Jo Lemoine cited earlier) includes special prayers for difficult and desperate cases. Here are some lines that might be especially helpful to widows: "At the hour of danger, at the time when my happiness and that of those dear to me was threatened, when my soul was afflicted and full of apprehension, I implored you. I begged you, whom everyone calls the saint of the impossible, the advocate of hopeless cases, the refuge at the final hour! I was never disappointed for having placed my trust in you. I come again to you now, no longer in tears of suffering, but with joy and serenity in my heart, to express my gratitude to you."[87]

## *Foundresses*

Many of the widow-saints were foundresses. Some — such as Saint Paula, Saint Frances of Rome, Saint Louise de Marillac, Blessed Marguerite d'Youville, and Conchita — are very well known and have been described elsewhere in this book. Others that you might want to research in depth include Saint Ethelreda (Audrey),

Blessed Clare of Rimini, Blessed Angeline Corbara, Saint Jeanne de Lestonnac, Saint Joaquina, Blessed Maria Domenica Brun Barbantini, and Mother María Luisa Josefa.

## Key Witnesses: Saint Jane de Chantal and Saint Elizabeth Seton

*The Witness of Saint Jane de Chantal* ❀ Of the many widow-saints we have described, Saint Jane (or Jeanne) de Chantal is one of the most intriguing. This is because of the many frustrations that stood in the way of Jane's conviction that she was meant to be a nun, even though she first had to stay in the world a long time to fulfill her duties as a mother of many children.

The information in this chapter is taken from *St. Jeanne de Chantal: Noble Lady, Holy Woman*, by André Ravier, S.J.,[88] and *Francis de Sales, Jane de Chantal: Letters of Spiritual Direction.*[89]

Jane de Chantal, who lived between 1572 and 1641, was born to a noble family of Burgundy lawyers. Because her mother died when Jane was still young, most of her education took place at the side of her father. From him she developed many analytical and administrative gifts that would prove useful to her in the order she would found later.

At the age of twenty, Jane married the Baron Christophe de Chantal. They enjoyed a most happy marriage and had six children, four of whom survived infancy. When her husband was killed in a hunting accident, Jane was devastated. For four months she was prostrate with grief. Soon Jane decided to take a private vow of chastity.[90]

Jane wanted to return to the house of her beloved father, but that was not the custom in those days. As described in an earlier chapter ("The Widow's Plight —

Ours and the Saints' "), the only way to provide security and social advantages for her children was to move into the home of her father-in-law. This tyrannical man demanded that Jane come to care for him. He threatened otherwise to marry his mistress and disinherit her children.

Life in this household was most difficult for Jane, since her father-in-law's mistress was the housekeeper, and there were five children of that union in the picture. The housekeeper tried to keep the devout and insightful Jane out of the management of her concerns. Marginalized, as we would say today, Jane made use of these circumstances, during her seven years at the house, to establish a kind of medical dispensary out of a wing of the manor house. So committed was Jane to tending the sick poor with her own hands that she herself contracted dysentery and became seriously ill, but fortunately she recovered.

During this time Jane was eaten up with the desire to do God's will. She became ill and emaciated from the stress, undergoing different phases of the purgative way.

Jane's spiritual life was an interior fire that burned ceaselessly, concealed by her sense of propriety, her practical activity, and her longing to please her loved ones. Her spiritual director did not really understand her. It was a great relief when she met Saint Francis de Sales in 1604. Accompanied by her father, Jane had gone to hear a series of Lenten sermons in Dijon.

Both Jane and Francis had independently received visions of each other, with God showing how the one would help the other one day. In his preface to the Paulist Press Spiritual Classics edition of *Francis de Sales, Jane de Chantal: Letters of Spiritual Direction*, Henri Nouwen remarks that the fruitfulness of this, one of the most famous spiritual friendships of the history of the Church, came about only because "Francis and Jane are not two lonely people who cling to each other in order to find a safe home in the midst of a fearful world. Both of them have found Jesus as the Bridegroom of their souls. He is the fulfillment of all their desires. He himself makes their friendship possible. They have been given to each other as spiritual friends, to enjoy each other's spiritual gifts, to support each other in their commitment to faithfulness, to be of mutual help in their search for perfection and to give shape to a new spiritual family in the Church."[91] It is Christ living in the center of the friendship that prevents possessiveness and allows for freedom of each individual to grow also in relationship to others.

After three years of spiritual direction, most of it by correspondence, Francis de Sales let Jane know that God had told him that she was the woman with whom he was to found a religious order of nuns. She was gradually to settle her children in life with the help of her extended family so that she would eventually be free to be a publicly consecrated woman.

Jane's interior life was to be purified by the forgiveness of the man who had accidentally shot her husband, by continual acts of abandonment to God's providence, and by frequent reception of the sacraments. She was to always think of her husband not as dead but as one "resting in the arms of God's mercy."

Most difficult of all was that while she yearned interiorly for a hidden cloistered life of prayer, circumstances made it necessary for her to stay in the world. She was to develop a perfect obedience to the will of God and to pray for an increase in faith that her dream would come true in spite of all the human reasons to doubt. She was moved to exclaim: "I tried to offer God my heart completely emptied of any wish but his pure, chaste love and obedience to him."[92]

Jane also had to struggle with her husband's family

who wanted her to solve her own problems and those of her children by a financially advantageous second marriage. Jane resisted with all her strength. "As much as I was able, I clung to the wood of the Cross, lest so many sweet siren songs tempt my soul to go soft and yield to the world's attractions."[93]

Finally, in 1610, Jane was able to leave her family and move to Annecy, the diocese where Francis de Sales was bishop, in order to form the new Order of the Visitation.

At first the idea was to found an order that would be both contemplative and active — the Sisters engaging in works of charity during part of the day. Admission to the order would not depend upon criteria common in that time for other communities, such as youth, health, and freedom from all family ties. The Visitation was to be more like a home — simple and modest and ascetical but always oriented to intimate love for God and for one another. They were to be gentle and tender, not so much occupied with great things but with doing little things with great love.[94] Saint Francis de Sales recommended that Jane correct the Sisters with affection and patience, without harshness or strong emotion.[95]

Problems with the canon law of the day led to the decision to keep the order completely cloistered and contemplative. In many ways Saint Jane de Chantal adapted Salesian spirituality to the needs of the feminine heart — perhaps so effectively because she had been a wife and mother first?[96]

Listen to this motherly voice in a letter written about a difficult nun: "Take good care of Sister Jeanne-Françoise; try to keep her as happy and busy as possible, and see to it that she eats well and gets enough sleep, for ordinarily an unstable mind is easily carried away by imaginary temptations. So, for that reason, dear Sister, be extremely compassionate, loving and patient with her. God and time will reveal to us what this is all about."[97]

During the next thirty-one years of her life, Jane went about establishing or supervising many convents of the new order, often through correspondence — eighty-seven in all! Riding sidesaddle throughout France, Jane was a dynamic foundress and guide for the souls in her charge.

It is fascinating to contrast two different oil paintings of our saint. In one she is recently widowed and in fancy dress. She looks miserable. The other one has Jane in her religious habit. She looks radiant, her eyes sparkling with joy.

Yet it is clear from her own writings and the letters of direction from Saint Francis de Sales that, for most of her life as a nun, she suffered from terrible spiritual dryness (a state in which one experiences a lack of feeling the love of Christ). Valiantly she responded to this, saying: "I never stop hoping in God, though he kill me, though he grind me into the dust of eternity."[98] She added, "I am attacked by each and every one of the temptations my spiritual daughters tell me about; God tells me what to say to them to console them, and then there I am, stuck with all those temptations and unable to help myself."[99]

As Jane grew older and saw her loved ones and companions pass away, she wrote, "Take my word for it — old age is miserable. My best friends have gone on to heaven and left me here on earth with all my sufferings; they were the good fruit, ready to be picked and placed on the King's banquet table, but I had to be left hanging on the vine because I was either too green or maybe rotten and full of worms."[100]

A month before Jane died, she experienced great peace by making a final examination of her whole life to a holy archbishop. She was happy to die, then, exactly when it pleased him.[101]

In spite of Jane's spiritual trials, she was so revered

for her love of God and neighbor that it became necessary on her visits to her different convents to stand with her back pressed closely to the wall when she was speaking, for her devotees used to try to get behind her to snip off pieces of her habit for relics!

Before Jane died, she urged the Visitation Sisters "to be in perfect unity with one another . . . [to] live together in all simplicity and preserve the integrity of perfect observance of the Rule."[102]

Jane's final words were: "I'm going, Jesus, Jesus, Jesus!"[103] On the day of her death, Saint Vincent de Paul saw a ball of fire rising from the earth and joining itself to a large circle, which was believed to be the soul of Saint Francis de Sales.

**The Witness of Saint Elizabeth Seton** ❀ Most of the information in this section is taken from the *Selected Writings from the Journal and Letters of Elizabeth Seton*,[104] as was the account on this great saint in an earlier part of this book.

As with many of our other saintly widows, Elizabeth Seton, the first American-born saint to be canonized (which was in 1975), fits into many categories. I have focused on her as a foundress because there is more information to be found on this than in the case of some of the other widow-foundresses, and also because of the delightful feature that she insisted that her children be part of the foundation!

Here is a thumbnail sketch of her life that I will follow by observations and quotations about her experience as a widow-foundress.

Born in 1774 to a prominent Episcopalian family of New York City, Elizabeth was quite young, probably three, when her mother, Catherine, died. She became much attached to her father, Richard, a doctor, and often accompanied him to Ellis Island to help the sickly poor immigrants on their arrival in the promised land. Even as an Episcopalian, Elizabeth was unusually devout and loved to pray, living from Sunday to Sunday for her spiritual enrichment. Yet the young woman was subject to despairing, even suicidal, moods over the evils of the world and her own miseries.[105]

Elizabeth married a charming young businessman, William Seton, and they had five children. Her happy family life was marred when her husband's business began to fail, leaving the family nearly bankrupt. This source of anxiety was followed by the fatal tuberculosis of her spouse. Hoping to save the life of her beloved husband, Elizabeth decided to take a trip with him and their eldest daughter to Leghorn (or Livorno) in Italy, supposed to be a better locale for a person with his health problems. Unfortunately, William's health became worse on the long journey, and he was quarantined in an Italian lazaretto before he died about six weeks later.

This tragedy was turned into a blessing because Elizabeth and her daughter were helped at this bleak time by her husband's Italian business associates and friends, the Filicchis, who were devout Catholics.

So beautiful were Elizabeth's impressions of the Catholic faith that, when she returned to New York, she was torn because the Church of her family and the one she was becoming more and more convinced had the greater claim to truth were both tugging at her. It was made clear to Elizabeth that if she became a Roman Catholic she would lose all the support she needed as a poor widow from her Episcopal relatives.

In fact, when she decided to become a Catholic, Elizabeth endured much persecution from her husband's family, especially since one of them wanted to follow her into her new religion. The previously wealthy widow found herself in comparative poverty, but she embraced the opportunity to live simply, doing the housework that a woman of her background would have had servants to perform. She was also happy to be free of social obligations she had never really liked in the first place.

Although Elizabeth loved the sacramental and devotional life of the Roman Catholic Church, she was surprised that there was so little educational opportunity for the children. She dreamed of starting her own little school for the poor. Eventually the widow's hopes were met with a similar idea on the part of the highly educated Bishop John Carroll of Baltimore. He invited her to start a teaching order for girls. This would be called The Sisters of Charity of Saint Joseph.

Elizabeth was thrilled with this idea, but she insisted that the bishop arrange things in such a way that her sons could be provided for at a flourishing Catholic school for boys and that her daughters could stay with her. The school curriculum of the first enterprise started under the auspices of the newly formed order included reading, writing, arithmetic, English, French, and needlework. As quite a number of the students were boarders, Elizabeth was busy from five-thirty in the morning until nine at night.

The motherhouse of the order and the school found their permanent foundation in Emmitsburg, Maryland, where there are still standing the original cottages that made up her convent and school.

The rule of life and daily routine of Elizabeth Seton's small order included Mass and prayer from six to eight in the morning, school at nine, dinner at one, school at three, then chapel at six-thirty during which time there was an examination of conscience and the Rosary was recited.

At the time of her death there would be Sisters of her order in Philadelphia and New York and plans for a Baltimore convent as well. Today there are six branches of these Sisters in many parts of the U.S. and Canada.

Elizabeth lived happily in the Lord despite the difficulties arising from poverty, heat, and cold that we would find daunting in the extreme.

Her worst sufferings involved the early painful deaths of her daughters and other beloved convert-relatives, and anxiety about the fate of her sons when they were out in the world after their schooling was completed.

It is wonderful that we have access to Elizabeth's intimate thoughts about the ups and downs of her life as wife, mother, widow, convert, nun, and foundress from the journals and letters she wrote to friends until her death in 1821.

The fact that her thoughts can be read in the original language and that she is so American in her personality make these letters particularly good reading for us. English-speaking women longing for holiness in the context of family life within a cultural milieu rather different from that of Catherine of Siena, Teresa of Ávila, or Thérèse of Lisieux find joy in our widow-saint's homey way of putting things.

I will now turn to specific quotations from Elizabeth Seton's journal and letters in the context of various phases of her life that reflect her experience of widowhood and also her life as a widow-foundress. (Keep in mind my earlier *caveat* about the inconsistencies, etc., in Elizabeth's writings.)

Less than a month after her husband's death she wrote to a dear friend: "I have written you some of the particulars of my dear William's departure, death I cannot call it, where the release is so happy as his was — it is my case that would be death to any one not supported by the Almighty Comforter, but his mercy has supported, and still upholds, and in it alone I trust."[106]

In a letter sent in November of 1806, Elizabeth confided in Bishop Carroll of Baltimore that from the earliest days of her acquaintance with the Faith she wished she could be a consecrated woman. Even before becoming a Catholic she envied Catholic nuns in Europe she read about in novels and admitted harboring "passionate wishes that there were such places in America as I read of in novels where people could be shut up from the world, and pray and be good always."[107] Evidently she had made private vows of a consecrated nature before.[108] Now, however, facing the possibility of her dear children being torn from their new faith by her anti-Catholic relatives should she not be able to supervise their lives, she could not think of being a Sister without finding some way to make sure the children were secure.

The first step toward her desired goal was accomplished when she was able to enroll her sons in a school for boys in Maryland in 1808. Best of all, she could be near a beautiful chapel she planned in the vicinity of her sons' school.

About the plans that circulated around her in clerical circles, she wrote in 1808: "I have invariably kept in the background and avoided even reflecting voluntarily on anything of the kind knowing that Almighty God alone could effect it if indeed it will be realized. . . . God will in his own time discover his intentions, nor will I allow one word of entreaty from my pen — His . . . blessed Will be done."[109]

The bishop decided that, even though she had young children still in her care, Elizabeth was the one to take charge of the projected order and school. She was delighted to be called "Mother" by so many of her new friends.[110]

The sufferings she herself had gone through made her heart full of empathy for those of others who would become consecrated women in her order. Consider the tone of a letter written to Cecilia, her convert relative (who would later join her in the order), suffering persecution at the hands of the New York City family members:

Yes, my Cecilia favored of Heaven, Associate of Angels, beloved Child of Jesus — You shall have the Victory, and He the Glory. To him be Glory forever who has called you to so glorious a combat, and so tenderly supports you through it. You will triumph, for it is Jesus who fights — not you my dear one — Oh so young and timid, weak, and irresolute, the Lamb could not stem a torrent, nor stand the beating storm — but the tender Shepherd takes it on his shoulder, casts his cloke about it, and the happy trembler finds itself at home before it knew its journey was half finished — and so my dear one it will be with you, He will not leave you one moment, nor suffer the least harm to approach you, not one tear shall fall to the ground nor one sigh of love be lost — happy, happy child — and if you are not removed to the sheltering fold that awaits you [in Elizabeth's home-convent-to-be] he will make you one in his own bosom until your task is done . . . how must [the saints] rejoice over you while walking so steadfastly in their paths, and their sufferings.[111]

By no means was the way smooth for the new congregation of Sisters. By 1809 Mother Seton was writing to Bishop Carroll of the difficulties that came when they were ordered by a cleric to give up the direction of a priest beloved by all the Sisters for his understanding and inspiration. Instead they were to be ordered about by a superior they thought did not enter into the spirit of their own plans. Saint Elizabeth was willing to accept for herself the cross of the many misunderstandings that took place at the beginning of the foundation but was not ready to see her Sisters suffer. For a while, another Sister was appointed to head the order, which was followed by much turmoil. Elizabeth was especially anxious concerning her right to have charge over her own children under the new circumstances. The Sister appointed as the congregation's head finally left, and the spirituality of the Sisters grew in peace and joy.[112]

Observe the sweet ironic humor of this account of the community Elizabeth wrote to her dear spiritual friend Antonio Filicchi, who was helping them financially as well as by his prayers: "Now then you will laugh when I tell you that your wicked little Sister is placed at the head of a Community of Saints, ten of the most pious Souls you could wish, considering that some of them are young and all under thirty. Six more postulents are daily waiting till we move in a larger place to receive them, and we might be a very large family if I received half who desire to come, but your Reverend Mother is obliged to be very cautious for fear we should not have the means of earning our living during the Winter. Yet as Sisters of Charity we should fear nothing. . . ."[113]

Here are some quotations from her instructions to her Sisters:[114]

◇ What should be our thoughts of this Body . . . a mass of matter to be destroyed in the destruction of all nature . . . and though by Faith we know that our body will be restored, yet it will be as by a new creation . . . so our bodies, as Sisters of Charity must be neither spared or looked at, no labours or sufferings considered for a moment but rather only asking what is this for my God! seeing everything only in that one view our God and our Eternity!

◇ The love of the Sisters for each other should be like that of our Lord which was gentle, benevolent and universal. . . .

◇ Have I learned to bear the weaknesses of others, they are obliged to bear with mine, and is it now very unreasonable that I should require from them indulgence for the many faults that escape me and

**118**

yet be unwilling to allow any to them. . . ?[115]

✧ Never be hurried by anything whatever — nothing can be more pressing than the necessity for your peace before God . . . you will help others more by the peace and tranquillity of your heart than by any eagerness or care you can bestow on them.[116]

✧ Take every day as a ring which you must engrave adorn and embellish with your actions, to be offered up in the evening at the altar of God.

✧ Mind not while in the body, what when out of the body you will have no need of.[117]

# Jesus: The Second Bridegroom

Perhaps at this stage of your reading you are feeling something like this: "How the widow-saints dealt with their new state of life is wonderful. I admire them. But I can't be that way. Maybe for a few hours a day, but all day? Come on! Most of the time I just feel desperate or depressed, or plain confused."

The holy widows did not get to be the way they were just by willing it or wishing it. It was because they opened themselves to Jesus as a Second Bridegroom in the depths of their hearts that they were able to respond fully to his leadings.

What does that mean? Some of us experience spectacular bridal graces, but many of us actually find our prayer life itself in crisis when we become widows.

First of all, I want you to realize that I am using the term "second bridegroom" in a general, wide sense. The way a saint like Elizabeth Seton would simply talk to Christ all day has quite a different emotional tone than we find in the explicitly bridal mysticism of a Blessed Angela of Foligno. As we shall see, Elizabeth expresses her confidence in Christ as her Sacred Bridegroom primarily by means of her trust in his providence in all circumstances. By contrast, in bridal mysticism of the traditional type, themes from the Song of Solomon (or Song of Songs) of the Old Testament of a sublimated erotic nature are linked to the notion of courtly love as found, for example, in the commentary on the Song of

Solomon by Saint Bernard of Clairvaux or the love poetry of Hadewijch.[1]

Conveying the mystical experience of Christ claimed by those who love him has always been a delicate if not impossible effort. It is so personal. It is my belief, as the author of many books touching on contemplative prayer (see especially *Prayers of the Women Mystics*), that our Second Bridegroom delights in wooing each of us in a way that is personal as well as classic. For instance, some women of prayer will witness how they found Christ in the sudden sight of a little violet by the road, because, say, they had always loved this flower, and so its sudden appearance at a time of depression was enough to reassure them of the love of Jesus. Another may only realize that she has a Second Bridegroom if the Lord appears in a vision and tells her so. Still others experience Christ's warm arms around them through the embrace of brothers and sisters in the family or Church.

Accordingly, in this chapter I will quote from some of our widow-saints about their experience of their Second Bridegroom, not so that you should hope for — or even demand! — the same treatment, as a test, but more that you would realize that Jesus does have the power to lift you, in a manner and time suitable to your own temperament, up to a new level of the Spirit, where your joy in him will be fuller.

I will begin with quotations about Jesus the Second Bridegroom as Savior, comforter, and protector, and save until later, passages about Jesus as lover.

## The Second Bridegroom as Savior, Comforter, and Protector

The passage of commentary from the prologue by Brother Arnaldo to *The Memorial* of Blessed Angela of Foligno[2] gives us a scriptural basis for the hope of the widow in Jesus as Savior, comforter, and protector: "Those who are truly faithful know what it is to probe, perceive, and touch the Incarnate Word of Life as he himself affirms in the gospel: 'If anyone loves me, he will keep my word, and my Father will love him, and we shall come to him and make our dwelling place with him.' And, 'He who loves, I will reveal myself to him' (John 14)."

Here in chronological order are some of the writings of our widow-saints introduced by a short statement by me of why I have included each one.

Sometimes from reading certain lush passages of bridal spirituality we can imagine that a widow need only make the decision to choose Jesus as the Second Bridegroom in order to experience perpetual bliss. The story of Saint Jane de Chantal gives us quite a different picture. Here we clearly see the Second Bridegroom not as a source of joy but still as the true Savior to whom all our sufferings are to be offered as a high "bridal" gift.

Writing about her time in the convent she says, "I write about God and talk of him as if I really know him, and most of the time I am sure I do know some things about him, and I do believe that there is great value in the pain and suffering I undergo every day, since I desire nothing else than this treasure of faith, hope and charity and the knowledge that I am doing everything I possibly can to find out what God wants me to do. . . ."[3]

So great were these interior sufferings that she could write: "I wish I were dead, because I am afraid that if it keeps on long enough I might stumble . . . how I wish at those times [of darkness] that I were already in Purgatory, where the only direction you can go is up, so that I can be sure I would eventually be reunited with God forever. . . . If I can keep from offending God in spite of all this, then I am content with whatever it may please him to allow me to suffer, even if I must suffer for the rest of my life; I want only to do it knowing that he wants me to, and that in suffering I am being faithful to him."[4]

Saint Vincent de Paul urged Saint Louise de Marillac and the Sisters of Charity they founded together to trust only in Christ as their protector. Is not the role of protector part the mission of the husband to the wife, and even more so the Second Bridegroom?

"Do you know what God does to a soul that is deprived of all human comfort and support?" he had asked. ". . . It is his pleasure to lead such a soul . . . and if she clings to Him with entire confidence, He will support her with His own hand and never let her sink." The author of the biography of Louise from which I have been quoting adds, "Louise . . . received the message with extraordinary tranquillity."[5]

During her husband's terrible illness aboard ship and then in quarantine, Saint Elizabeth Seton wrote her friend that during the terrible nights when he was struggling to breathe, "If I could forget my God one moment at these times I should go mad — but He hushes all — Be still and know that I am God your Father." In the same letter about anticipating the loss of her husband she writes: "If we do not meet again here — there we shall be separated no more — if I have lost them now, their gain is infinite and eternal. How often I tell my W [her husband, William] 'when you awake in that world you will find nothing could tempt you to return to this, you will see that your care over your wife and little ones, was like a hand only to hold the cup which God himself will give if he takes you.' "[6]

After becoming a widow, Elizabeth was much consoled by the comfort to be found in faith and trust in Christ as her Second Bridegroom. In one of her first letters after the death of her husband she confides in her reader that her life would be death without the help of God, her comforter.[7]

"It pleased God to try me very hard in many ways — but also to bestow such favors and comforts that it would be worse than disobedience not to dwell on his Mercy while I must bow to his dispensations."[8] She found great comfort always in the thought of the joy of eternity and turned her grief about the death of not only her husband but of other loved ones into hope and joy in the thought of the delights of heaven.[9]

As we also need to do, our American saint flung herself at the feet of her Heavenly Spouse, seeking in him the happiness she had lost from the death of her husband: "Suffer me to remain at thy Feet. There it is that I find my happiness O Divine JESUS! — my Joy, my Delight, that Peace of God. . . ."[10]

Saint Elizabeth saw Christ, the Second Bridegroom, also as her protector as a widow and mother of children. Right after the death of her husband she writes about "my dear Fatherless children — Fatherless to the world, but rich in God their Father for he will never leave us nor forsake us. . . ."[11]

When she was fearful of her future, her friend Antonio Filicchi told Elizabeth, "My little Sister, God, the Almighty, is laughing at you; he takes care of little birds and makes the lilies grow, and you fear he will not take care of you — I tell you he will take care of you."[12]

In her journal, Elizabeth wrote: "My saviour My Jesus hide me — shelter me shelter the shuddering trembling soul and lays itself in thy hand."[13]

She continued: "Look up my soul, fear not, the love which nourishes us is unchangable as Him from whom it proceeds — it will remain when every other sentiment will vanish — and could we desire more than to draw continual refreshment from a stream so near the fountain head — so pure so sweet a stream![14]

One aspect of this widow's trust in Christ as her protector was Elizabeth Seton's sense of the faith itself with its firm teachings. Here is one of the homey images she used in a letter to her closest friend who was not a Catholic: "Peace, my dear. . . . We will jog up the hill as quietly as possible, and when the flies and mosquitos bite, wrap the cloak round and never mind them; they can only penetrate the surface. Darling Julia, how I wish you would have such a Catholic cloak also."[15]

Reading her words at times of insecurity I am encouraged: ". . . the most painful things in the order of his providence can increase our confidence and Peace in him, since all will draw us but nearer to himself if we only kiss his hand as that of the best of Fathers."[16]

How humorously she writes of her own approaching death: ". . . the carcase is going to the dung hill to wait for the Resurrection."[17]

Studying the biography of Concepción Cabrera de Armida, or Conchita, we find a special way of encountering Christ as the Bridegroom-Savior — being drawn oneself into union with Christ's saving passion. The description to follow may provide you with a poignant sense of how far he could be leading each of us also if we were sufficiently generous of heart.

Shortly before the feast of the Annunciation, when Conchita was forty years old, Jesus began to prepare her in prayer for what she says he called the "mystical incarnation." During a retreat, before the feast, Conchita felt great anguish for the salvation of souls. She made a general confession of all the faults of her life.

Then, on the morning of the feast, after a night spent in prayer and penance, at Mass she felt herself taken over by the presence of Christ, who said to her: "Here I am, I want to incarnate Myself mystically in your heart. . . . Receive Me. . . . I have taken possession of your heart. . . ."[18]

She asked if this was the spiritual marriage. He replied: "Much more than that. Marriage is a form of more external union; the grace of incarnating Me, of living and growing in your soul, never to leave it, to possess you and to be possessed by you as in one and the same substance, without, obviously, you giving Me life; rather, it is I who communicate it to your soul in a compenetration which cannot be comprehended: it is the grace of graces. . . . It is a union of the same nature as that of the union of heaven, except that in paradise the veil which conceals the Divinity disappears. . . ."[19]

Conchita felt a sublime sense of Christ living in her soul, but she asked just the same: " 'Lord, what if this was a figment of my imagination or a delusion?' He replied, 'You will discern all that from the results flowing therefrom . . . no one merits it. Love Me. This kind of union is most profound, most intimate and, if your soul remains faithful, it will be an internal union.' "[20]

Conchita wrote that, after this experience, "I felt my spirit inundated with freshness, peace, infinite delights, but was it true? Yes, certainly, year after year I saw myself humiliated by this promise which apparently was never carried out. I did not understand it all. My tears flowed. . . . Behold, the handmaid of the Lord. Be it done unto me according to Thy Word."[21]

The form that this mystical incarnation was to take was to urge Conchita on to be a victim for the Church in union with Christ — Priest and Host. It was to be a path of suffering, lived in fidelity to each inspiration of the Holy Spirit. She was to offer herself on the altar in union with Christ, through which thousands and thousands of souls will be saved. Her biographer writes: "This mystical incarnation eminently realized the 'royal priesthood' of all the members of the family of Christ."[22]

Those readers interested in exploring the implications of such a vocation might want to get a copy of *Before the Altar*,[23] the Eucharistic Adoration meditations Conchita wrote for members of the orders she co-founded, a beloved text now for many lay Eucharistic Adoration Catholics throughout the world.

## The Second Bridegroom as Lover

In the foreword to *Angela of Foligno: Complete Works* we read these words: "The marrow of Angela's inner life, her passionate love affair with the suffering God-man."[24] For example, after her initial reconversion as a penitent, Angela stripped herself of all her clothing and stood before a crucifix pledging perpetual chastity.

The Holy Spirit told this Italian widow: "I will hold you closely to me and much more closely than can be observed with the eyes of the body."[25]

So important for a widow who no longer has someone close to enjoy and appreciate her is this locution Blessed Angela heard on the road from Assisi to Foligno. Jesus said: "Your whole life, your eating, drinking, sleeping, and all that you do are pleasing to me."[26]

Here is Angela's account of the sense of intimacy that came after her return from the pilgrimage that marked an entrance into still more mystical states of union: "Once I was back home, I felt so peaceful and was so filled with divine sweetness that I find no words to express my experience; and there was also in me a desire to die." (She wanted to reach the source of this happiness and at the same time was afraid of losing it.) "I lay at home enthralled by this great consolation and in a state of languor for eight days." Angela understood that she was not only listening to Christ but feeling him within her. "You do not see me but you feel me."[27]

Jesus called her "my temple, my delight." And "you are holding the ring of my love. From now on you are engaged to me and you will never leave me."[28]

Blessed Angela smelled delightful fragrances during this time. Her companion saw her in ecstasy, during which she radiated incredible colors and even a star.

An especially bridal-sounding mystical moment occurred while Blessed Angela was meditating on the crucifixion, and Christ showed her his throat and his arms.

Her sorrow was turned into an intense joy. She felt she was seeing his divinity through this sight. Sometimes she would see a supernatural brightness, with her bodily eyes, greater than that of the sun, at the elevation of the Host during Mass.[29] Sometimes she saw large eyes in the Host of the same kind of ineffable beauty.

On a different occasion Christ told Angela that she was full of God, who was embracing her soul. During such experiences she says that "all the members of my body thrilled with delight."[30]

In spite of all these strong experiences, Angela still had doubts. She asked Christ for a sign for herself alone. Jesus said that the sort of sign she was asking for she could still doubt, but that he would give her a better one: "I deposit in you a love of me so great that your soul will be continually burning for me," and that this love would be so great that she would actually welcome offenses and deal with them patiently.[31] And in fact this sign did take place.

I want to pause here a moment. No matter what doubts we might have about the flamboyant mysticism of saints like Angela, how can we doubt but that it requires tremendous grace to avoid all bitterness and to become patient with all the little difficulties of daily life? May all of us pray for such a sign that we are beloved of the Second Bridegroom!

Christ also told Angela that he had to hide some of the love he had for her that she might be able to bear it. So great was his love that he could not remember her sins and faults. All God wants in return for his love is our love. He explained that if he showed her this love she would no longer hunger for him, for in this life he wanted her to desire him and languish for him.[32]

Experiencing Christ as the Bridegroom in the sense of his being the true lover of her heart and soul was for Saint Jane de Chantal mediated by the spontaneity of the love for herself she found in the friendship of the holy Saint Francis de Sales. In extending to her a pledge of service to help her to spiritual growth in her distressing circumstances as a widow living in worldly and sinful surroundings, he expressed himself with compelling ardor: "I am all yours. . . . God has given me to you; so consider me as yours in Him, and call me whatever you like; it makes no difference."[33]

For someone accustomed to natural human love as a happily married woman, opening to this distinctly Christian but ardently overflowing love from a holy man seems to have been the key to the new spirituality she was called to embrace. Before this friendship, Jane's way to God was somewhat stiff and formal even though characterized by surrender of the will and total commitment to executing the will of God in prayer and love of neighbor. De Sales recommended instead walking in the presence of God with absolute liberty of spirit.

By freedom of spirit, of course, De Sales did not mean "freedom to sin." What he wanted Jane to know was more joy in her Second Bridegroom, because he was convinced that no deprivation can sadden the heart that belongs wholly to God. Little inconveniences or trifles do not upset such a Christian. Interruptions make no difference. Those with liberty of spirit are rarely angry and almost always serene.[34]

It is my belief that, enchanted by the ever-so-personal love of Francis for her whole person as a woman of God, Jane could allow herself to be receptive to Christ the Second Bridegroom in quite a new way.

In her own letters of spiritual direction, Jane de Chantal could recommend that "the great method of prayer is to have no method at all. When the Holy Spirit has taken possession of the person who prays, it does as it pleases without any more need for rules and methods. . . . Prayer must happen by grace not by artfulness."[35]

Yet, characteristically, there comes a time on the path of total surrender to Jesus when even attachment to holy people has to give way to complete reliance on Christ alone. Francis promised Jane that one day he would detach her even from himself. It was painful for the woman in her to find that the duties of the archbishop and Church diplomat often kept her saint far away from his home base. Wendy Wright in the book *Bond of Perfection* and also in her introduction to the Paulist Press edition of *Francis de Sales, Jane de Chantal: Letters of Spiritual Direction* emphasizes the fact that "as a woman shaped by marriage and motherhood, she [Jane de Chantal] felt the psychic rightness of continually dwelling in the embrace of a fully realized relationship." Yet she accepted the sacrifice and struggled to reduce all her desires to the desire for unity with God in acceptance of his will. This is a kind of bridal spiritual nakedness in relationship to Jesus the Second Bridegroom.[36]

At the time of the death of her dear spiritual friend Francis de Sales, our French widow-saint replied to a letter of condolence from her brother with the following words:

> You say you want to know what my heart felt on that occasion. Ah, it seems to me that it adored God in the profound silence of its terrible anguish. Truly, I have never felt such an intense grief nor has my spirit ever received so heavy a blow . . . the only thing that is left to console me is to know that it is my God that has done this, or at least, has permitted this blow to fall. Alas. My heart is too weak to support this heavy burden. . . . Yes, my God, you put this beautiful soul into the world, now you have taken it back . . . may the name of the Lord be blessed. . . . I affirm what it has pleased Him to do — to take from us that great flame that lit up this miserable world and let it shine in his

kingdom. . . . I am certainly too insignificant to merit such a great blessing as well as the contentment that I had in seeing my soul held in the hands of such a great man who was truly a man of God.[37]

In her much more austere fashion, Saint Louise de Marillac liked to talk about her union in prayer with her Second Bridegroom as "the interior solitude of the heart." Saint Louise once wrote to Saint Vincent de Paul that her heart was "radiant with joy." Such words console us, especially, when we remember that Louise was of a melancholy temperament inclined to fear and guilt.[38]

Here is how Blessed Marie of the Incarnation describes her sense of Christ the Second Bridegroom as lover: "It is impossible to say how agonizing this love is and yet the soul has no desire to free itself, except to possess him whom she loves. It seems to it that it has spiritual arms which are constantly extended to embrace him. . . . All its sighing, all its attention, even its life are constantly in this state of predilection for its well-beloved. . . . I cannot explain to what the Beloved reduces the soul in order to make it pursue him all the more. He secures it by double chains. He holds it captive under his own loving laws and despoils it completely in order to make it follow him."[39]

All this yearning prepared Marie of the Incarnation of Tours, France, for the mystical marriage with Christ that took place some eight years after she was widowed: "Then, engulfed in the presence of this adorable Majesty, Father, Son, and Holy Spirit, adoring him in the awareness and acknowledgement of my lowliness, the Sacred Person of the Divine Word revealed to me that he was in truth the spouse of the faithful soul. I understood this truth with absolute certainty and this very understanding became the imminent preparation for this grace to be effected in me. At that moment, this ador-

able Person seized my soul and embracing it with inde-
scribable love united it to himself, taking it as his spouse."
She went on to say: "Hithereto [the soul] had been in
continual longing and expectation. . . . Now the soul has
no further longing because it possesses him whom it
loves. The soul is all his."[40]

For Saint Elizabeth Seton, as for many a woman, the
transition to experiencing Christ as her true love involved
having to face limitations that Church law and the meta-
physics of finite love placed to being satisfied with male
human love. Evidently the special love she had for her
married friend and protector Antonio Filicchi — while
returned from his side in essence — did not match hers
when it came to the amount of time Elizabeth spent on
correspondence and Antonio's own precautions but also
lack of time for such writings. Struggles with the feeling
of neglect are a rather constant theme in the correspondence. Evidently sometimes he didn't send her a new
address as he traveled about, as can be seen from this
excerpt: "You said you would not write yet if it had been
in your power you would have sent at least your direction [address]. Often my heart cries out to God for you
and if I did not commit you wholly to him I should be
very unhappy."[41]

Sometimes she was able to deal with her disappointment in not hearing from him as often as she wished
with a charming humor: "Tonino, Tonino [Antonio's nick-
name] — how I long to meet you in your state of perfection, where I shall receive the transfusion of your affections without your exertions. . . ."[42]

As a spiritual friend he became a soul mate to her,
and she experienced the pain of the fact that as a married man he could never be part of her daily life in the
way she would have loved. This is expressed quite sub-
tly, for she was clearly aware of the dangers of drawing
him too close to her under the circumstances. He did

not encourage her to write to him on his business travels too often.[43]

In a letter to him she wrote: "I begin now wishfully to watch every evening hoping . . . for a letter from — this you may think childish dear Antonio but remember you have not a female heart, and mine is most truely and fondly attached to you, as you have proved when I have been most contradictory and troublesome to you — fearing too much not to possess your invaluable affection."[44]

And then, in another plaintive letter she said that "if I was your brother, Antonio I would never leave you for one hour — but as it is I try rather to turn every affection to God, well knowing that there alone their utmost exercise cannot be misapplied and most ardent hopes can never be disappointed."[45]

Such sufferings of loneliness only led Elizabeth the more to realize that, for her, Jesus could be her only Bridegroom as a widow, "but considering with my own heart, its errors, its wanderings and still added sorrows which all call to it with an irresistible force to give itself to God alone, I ask why . . . even lend it to the uncertain influences of human affections, why allow it to look for Antonio to be made happy by his attentions or disturbed by his neglects — when those moments spent in writing to or thinking of my brother are given to my J [Jesus]. . . . He never disappoints me but repays every instant with hours of sweet Peace and unfailing contentment — and the tenderest interest you even can bestow on me is only a stream of which he is the fountain. . . . This on my part — on yours, the multiplicity of business, laziness of temper, diffidence of disposition, inconvenience in writing English with other etcetera's are an all sufficient acknowledgement however delicately expressed, that writing to your Sister must be a sacrifice which her affection for you would rather dispense with than constrain you to perform."[46]

And this from another letter after receiving a loving one from Antonio: "I should wish earnestly my most dear Brother never to think of you with tenderness but when calling on Almighty God to bless you, then often my heart overflows and exhausts the sighs and tears of affection which at all other times are not carefully repressed — and far from feeling less interest for you and less value for your affection it has never so earnestly so anxiously prayed for you as during the few weeks past in which it has been pained by your neglect. . . ."[47]

How lovable must this widow have been who, in this vulnerable a manner, was able to write to her happily married friend: "Dear dear Antonio why must I speak to you in a manner so little conformed to the feelings of my heart — but you know yourself drew the line, and the kindness and sweetness of affection must be vailed — from the searcher of hearts it cannot, and it delights me to consider that he also sees its sincerity, simplicity and holiness."[48]

Looking back we can see how the movements of what she herself called "my inflammable heart" were a preparation for her complete self-surrender to Christ in her religious vows.

"Many seek to love God by different methods but there is none so short and so easy as to do everything for his love, to set this seal on all our actions, and keep ourselves in his presence by the commerce of the heart with him in full simplicity without embarrassment or disguise."[49]

In a certain way, contrasting the flavor of this passage with that of the passionate writings of some other widow-saints, we could say that Elizabeth experienced Christ not so much as Second Bridegroom but as Second Husband, like a spouse in a long-term relationship, always near at hand.

Even before becoming a widow, Conchita experienced

a mystical marriage with Christ. If you recall, this took place after fulfilling her burning desire to engrave the name of Jesus on her breast.

"It seems to me that with the monogram, the Lord opened a door to lavish on me His graces. From that day on how He pursued me! What attention! What tenderness! What astounding kindness toward a miserable creature such as I! He never left me alone neither by day nor by night, neither when I was praying nor when I was not. He kept telling me 'I want you to be all Mine! You are Mine now but I want you to be even more so Mine!' He said over and over: 'Come, I want to be spiritually married to you. . . .' "[50]

I end this section with this question for myself and for you, my readers: "Why not invite Jesus to be my Second Bridegroom? Do I think that he cannot want me because I am old, ugly, worn-out, sinful?" The accounts of the widow-saints make it plain that God's taste does not exclude such shortcomings. What will it be like when we arrive at the Day of Judgment to find out that Jesus wanted to lavish on us his most intimate love, but we were too caught up in our own self-hatred or depression to let him in?

# Mary: The Exalted Widow

In a certain way it seems odd to think of Mary, the Mother of the Infant Jesus, as also his Bride, but indeed we know that it is so. Who could have a more intimate relationship to Christ, the Second Bridegroom, than the woman whose heart was unscarred by sin, and whose whole earthly life was spent in union with him?

Would it be wrong or inappropriate to say that Mary's famous words when proclaiming her grace to her cousin Elizabeth also apply to her widowhood? "He has put down the mighty from their thrones, and exalted those of low degree" (Luke 1:52).

We can forget that Mary was a widow. No matter how unusual her marriage was, we know it must have been the most sublime in terms of union of hearts. How Mary must have grieved to have been deprived of the daily companionship of the one man, save Jesus himself, who understood fully about her immaculate conception and the miraculous birth and destiny of their Son!

The picture of Mary's life as a widow, after the death of Joseph, and as a bereaved mother after the ascension of Jesus, includes features characteristic of each of the paths of our widowed saints. Surely she was constantly exercising a motherly ministry to the needy of the Church family and for all those in suffering. Surely she was a penitent in the sense not of making up for her own sins but as offering her own pain for redemptive graces to pour down on the Church. Surely she had the soul of a nun, her heart a closed garden in her mystical communion with the Christ whose own heart was best understood by his mother. Surely she came up against all the evils in the early Church with a fearless prophetic spirit. Surely she counts in her role as mediatrix of all graces the role of a foundress of the community we call the Church.

I also think of Mary from heaven as exercising a widow-to-widow ministry with our saintly widows! Blessed Angela claims that it was the Virgin Mary who obtained for her the grace of conversion from her relatively tepid state before that moment of ecstasy.[1] Saint Louise de Marillac urged the Sisters of Charity "to take the Blessed Virgin as your only Mother."[2]

Elizabeth Seton, before her conversion, realized that Mary could not help loving and pitying the poor souls her Son died for. She wrote: "I felt really I had a Mother which you know my foolish heart so often laments to have lost in early days — from the first remembrance of infancy I have looked in all the plays of childhood and wildness of youth to the clouds for my Mother, and at that moment it seemed as if I had found more than her . . . so I cried myself to sleep on her heart." In her journal we find this prayer: "O my Blessed Mother Obtain from Him what is necessary for my coming to Him — that I may one day possess Him with You — for Eternity."[3]

Right after being widowed, Conchita used to pray the *Memorare* to Mary ending with, "Mary, help me and my eight orphans."[4] During the last twenty years of her life after her children were grown, she said Jesus told her: "There remains for you to pass the last stage of your life imitating My Mother for obtaining graces for the Works of the Cross. . . . Carry on your mission, imitate the virtues of Mary in her solitude, virtues which brought about Her union with Me, Her obedience to My will and Her desire of heaven."[5]

I do not think that it is an accident that so many widows find themselves in church each day after Mass praying the mysteries of the Rosary, so full of pain, but also of joy and glory. For where is the joy and glory of a widow but in the hope that she will one day experience the mysteries of her faith fulfilled in an eternity of happiness?

After becoming a widow myself, someone gave me a card with a picture of Mary accompanied by the following words:

> Maria Excelsa Vidua
> Maria Excelsa Vidua
> Mary Exalted Widow
> Pray for us.

Inside is a prayer to Mary, Exalted Widow, which translated roughly, includes these words:

> O Mary, conceived without original sin,
> I pray . . . for the gift of spiritual peace. . . .
> You whose heart was pierced by a sword,
> as prophesied by Simon at the presentation
> of Jesus in the Temple,
> to whom was prophesied by the widow Anna,
> who suffered the death of your holy spouse,
>    Joseph,
> you who stood at the foot of the cross,
> contemplating the death of your Son
> for sinners, and accepted the plan of the Father,
> I pray that you would intercede for me,
> that with your example of supreme faith,
> I would accept the will of the Lord,
> in the hope of receiving the grace to be reunited
> with everyone in his holy kingdom. Amen.

# Conclusion

A few notes about my own life during the writing of *A Widow's Walk.*

When I started my research I was hoping to join a lay community. My dear spiritual friend and mentor Charles Rich, then ninety-six years old, himself a consecrated lay contemplative, told me that if I asked for the grace, God would give me the heart of a nun. I made a perfunctory prayer to appease him, but thought little of it, so eager was I to continue my search for a second husband.

After starting to write about the widow-saints, however, something strange began to happen. I was praying to these saints to help me with the book and also with my own life. Gradually I began to feel a sense of peace with the idea that perhaps I was meant to consecrate my heart to Christ alone.

The Holy Spirit reminded me of a locution I had received soon after becoming a widow concerning a community called the Handmaids of Nazareth. These are women of any age who wish to be Sisters. Some will live in a house of adoration, but others may remain wherever they are presently dwelling, in order to take care of children, relatives, etc. They communicate by phone or FAX and meet at gatherings and retreats.

For a year and a half I tried to fit into this community. I loved the foundress, and I loved being a consecrated woman wearing a simple blue dress. I did find that my consecration with a private vow, pending final vows in the community, gave me a new sense of bridal intimacy with Christ and a focus very different from that of an ardent lay apostle. Nevertheless, it seemed to me that I was not meant for communal life, even at a distance.

I am still in communication with the foundress and I am happy to recommend it to other widows (single, divorced, or whose marriages have been annulled) who might not feel suited to communities who only take younger people, or only those who can live in a convent. The FAX number is 716-248-2469, Handmaids of Nazareth.

Presently, instead, I am starting a movement called Women and Men of Jesus. It is designed to give shape to the prayer life of Catholics, especially those who are semi- or completely retired and want to devote the rest of their lives to the Church. Women and Men of Jesus who have made private vows of celibacy, or wish to, may choose to wear simple blue clothing as a sign of their dedication. For more information send me a letter or postcard. The address is: Ronda Chervin, 115 Yonder Lane, Sedona, AZ 86336. Enclose a stamped self-addressed envelope. Or call and ask me to return the call collect. I am at 520-204-6406; my FAX number is 520-204-5547.

# Bibliography

Angela of Foligno, Blessed. *Angela of Foligno: Complete Works.* Translated with an Introduction by Paul Lachance, O.F.M. (New York: Paulist Press, 1993).

Biersack, Louis, O.F.M. Cap., *The Saints and Blessed of the Third Order of Saint Francis* (Paterson, N.J.: Saint Anthony Guild Press, 1943).

Cabrera de Armida, Concepción. *Conchita: A Mother's Spiritual Diary.* Edited by M. M. Philipon, O.P. Translated by Aloysius J. Owen, S.J. (Staten Island, N.Y: Alba House, 1978).

Chervin, Martin. *Children of the Breath* (Oak Lawn, Ill.: C.M.J., 1998).

Chervin, Ronda De Sola. *Treasury of Women Saints* (Ann Arbor, Mich.: Servant Publications, 1991).

_____, *En Route to Eternity — The Story of My Life* (Highland, N.Y.: Miriam Press, 1994).

do Robeck, Nesta. *Saint Elizabeth of Hungary* (Milwaukee, Wisc.: The Bruce Publishing Co., 1954).

Fitts, Mary Pauline, G.N.S.H. *Hands to the Needy: Mother d'Youville, Apostle to the Poor* (New York: Doubleday and Co., 1950).

*Francis de Sales, Jane de Chantal: Letters of Spiritual Direction.* Translated by Peronne Marie Thibert, V.H.M. Selected and introduced by Wendy M. Wright and Joseph F. Poer, O.S.F.S. Preface by Henri J. M. Nouwen (New York: Paulist Press, 1988).

Jorgensen, Johannes. *Saint Bridget of Sweden.* Vol. II. Translated by Ingebord Lund (New York: Longmans Green and Co., 1954).

Lemoine, Jo. *Rita: The Saint of the Impossible.* Translated by Florestine Audette, R.J.M. (Boston: St. Paul Books and Media, 1992).

*Marie of the Incarnation: Selected Writings.* Edited by

Irene Mahoney, O.S.U. (New York: Paulist Press, 1989).

Olive, Martin-Maria, O.P. *Praxedes: Wife, Mother, Widow and Lay Dominican* (Rockford, Ill.: TAN Books and Publishers, 1987).

Ravier, André, S.J. *St. Jeanne de Chantal: Noble Lady, Holy Woman.* Translated by Mary Emily Hamilton (San Francisco: Ignatius Press, 1989).

*Saint Catherine of Genoa: Life and Sayings.* Translated and edited by Paul Garvin (Staten Island, N.Y.: Alba House, 1964).

Seton, Saint Elizabeth. *Selected Writings from the Journal and Letters of Elizabeth Seton.* Edited by Ellin Kelly and Annabelle Melville (New York: Paulist Press, 1987).

Thurston, Bonnie Bowman. *The Widows: A Women's Ministry in the Early Church* (Minneapolis: Fortress Press, 1989).

Von Hildebrand, Alice. *By Grief Refined* (Steubenville, Ohio: Franciscan University Press, 1994).

Woodgate, M. V. *St. Louise de Marillac: Foundress of the Sisters of Charity* (St. Louis: B. Herder Book Co., 1942).

# Chapter Notes

## Introduction

1. Martin Chervin, *Children of the Breath* (Oak Lawn, Ill.: C.M.J., 1998).
2. Ronda De Sola Chervin, *En Route to Eternity — The Story of My Life* (Highland, N.Y.: Miriam Press, 1994).

## The Widow's Plight — Ours and the Saints'

1. Ronda De Sola Chervin, *Treasury of Women Saints* (Ann Arbor, Mich.: Servant Publications, 1991), p. 70.
2. *Conchita: A Mother's Spiritual Diary*, edited by M. M. Philipon, O.P., translated by Aloysius J. Owen, S.J. (Staten Island, N.Y.: Alba House, 1978), p. 8.
3. Ibid., p. 9.
4. Ibid., p. 34.
5. See *Rita: The Saint of the Impossible*, by Jo Lemoine, translated by Florestine Audette, R.J.M. (Boston: St. Paul Books and Media, 1992), pp. 29-30.
6. See *Hands to the Needy: Mother d'Youville, Apostle to the Poor*, by Mary Pauline Fitts, G.N.S.H. (New York: Doubleday and Co., 1950).
7. Ibid., p. 48ff.
8. Ibid., p. 53.
9. Ibid., p. 55.
10. Ibid., pp. 57-58.
11. Ibid., p. 59.
12. Ibid., p. 60.
13. Ibid., pp. 64-65.
14. *Saint Catherine of Genoa: Life and Sayings*, translated and edited by Paul Garvin (Staten Island, N.Y.: Alba House, 1964).
15. Ibid., p. 23.
16. Blessed Angela of Foligno, *Angela of Foligno: Com-*

*plete Works*, translated with an Introduction by Paul Lachance, O.F.M. (New York: Paulist Press, 1993), p. 126.
17. Ibid., p. 143.
18. Saint Elizabeth Seton, *Selected Writings from the Journal and Letters of Elizabeth Seton*, edited by Ellin Kelly and Annabelle Melville (New York: Paulist Press, 1987), p. 100.
19. Ibid., p. 127.
20. Ibid., p. 130.
21. Ibid., p. 178.
22. *Conchita. . .* , pp. 49-50.
23. Ibid., p. 51.
24. Ibid., pp. 51-52.
25. Ibid., p. 53.
26. Ibid., p. 106.
27. Ibid., p. 107.
28. Alice Von Hildebrand, *By Grief Refined* (Steubenville, Ohio: Franciscan University Press, 1994).
29. *Conchita. . .* , p. 53.
30. Ibid., p. 103.
31. See *Treasury of Women Saints*, pp. 247-248.
32. Ibid., pp. 52-53.
33. Johannes Jorgensen, *Saint Bridget of Sweden*, translated by Ingebord Lund (New York: Longmans Green and Co., 1954), Vol. II, p. 56.
34. Ibid., Vol. II, p. 42.
35. Ibid.
36. Ibid., Vol. II, p. 70.
37. Ibid., Vol. II, p. 90.
38. *Francis de Sales, Jane de Chantal: Letters of Spiritual Direction*, translated by Peronne Marie Thibert, V.H.M.; selected and introduced by Wendy M. Wright and Joseph F. Poer, O.S.F.S.; Preface by Henri J. M. Nouwen (New York: Paulist Press, 1988), p. 210.
39. Ibid., p. 216.

40. Ibid., pp. 216-217.

41. Ibid., p. 217.

42. André Ravier, S.J., *St. Jeanne de Chantal: Noble Lady, Holy Woman*, translated by Mary Emily Hamilton (San Francisco: Ignatius Press, 1989) p. 93.

43. *Francis de Sales. . .* , p. 136.

44. Ibid.

45. M. V. Woodgate, *St. Louise de Marillac: Foundress of the Sisters of Charity* (St. Louis: B. Herder Book Co., 1942), p. 88.

46. Ibid., p. 221ff.

47. *Selected Writings from the Journal. . .* , p. 98.

48. Ibid., p. 282.

49. *Conchita. . .* , pp. 77-78.

50. Ibid., p. 57.

51. Ibid., see pp. 79-81.

52. Ibid., p. 91.

53. Ibid., pp. 95-97.

54. Ibid., p. 99.

55. Ibid., p. 106.

56. *Saint Bridget of Sweden*, p. 102ff.

57. *St. Louise de Marillac. . .* , p. 34.

58. *Marie of the Incarnation: Selected Writings*, edited by Irene Mahoney, O.S.U. (New York: Paulist Press, 1989) p. 10.

59. Ibid., p. 12ff.

60. *Selected Writings from the Journal. . .* , p. 171.

61. Ibid., see pp. 179-180.

62. Ibid., p. 171.

63. Ibid., p. 185.

64. Ibid., p. 186.

65. Ibid., p. 189.

66. Ibid., p. 193.

67. Ibid., p. 201.

68. Ibid., p. 288.

69. Ibid., p. 294.

70. Louis Biersack, O.F.M. Cap., *The Saints and Blessed of the Third Order of Saint Francis* (Paterson, N.J.: Saint Anthony Guild Press, 1943), p. 71.

71. *Hands to the Needy. . . ,* p. 69.

72. *Selected Writings from the Journal. . . ,* see p. 189.

73. Ibid., p. 193.

74. Ibid., see p. 278.

75. *Conchita. . . ,* p. 248.

76. *Angela of Foligno: Complete Works,* p. 47.

77. Ibid., p. 19.

78. Ibid., see p. 23.

79. Ibid., p. 143.

80. Ibid., p. 21.

81. Ibid., p. 18.

82. Ibid., p. 141.

83. *Francis de Sales. . . ,* p. 4.

84. Ibid., p. 124.

85. Ibid., see p. 42.

86. Ibid., p. 45.

87. Ibid., see p. 39.

88. Ibid., p. 190.

89. Ibid., p. 169.

90. *Hands to the Needy. . . ,* see p. 70ff.

91. Ibid., p. 79.

92. Ibid., p. 83.

93. *Selected Writings from the Journal. . . ,* p. 98.

94. Ibid., p. 100.

95. Ibid., see p. 142.

96. Ibid., p. 181.

97. *Conchita. . . ,* pp. 55-57.

98. Ibid., p. 56.

99. Ibid., p. 58.

100. See *The Widows: A Women's Ministry in the Early Church,* by Bonnie Bowman Thurston (Minneapolis: Fortress Press, 1989), pp. 62-63.

101. Ibid.
102. Ibid., p. 9.
103. Ibid., p. 13.
104. Ibid., p. 24.
105. Ibid., p. 28.
106. Ibid., p. 29.
107. Ibid., see p. 30ff.
108. Ibid., p. 50.
109. Ibid., p. 62.
110. Ibid., p. 67.
111. Ibid., p. 71.
112. Ibid., p. 107.
113. Ibid., p. 74.
114. Ibid., p. 89.
115. Ibid., p. 90.
116. Ibid., pp. 96-97.
117. Ibid., pp. 98-99.
118. Ibid., pp. 101-102.
119. *Selected Writings from the Journal. . .*, p. 126.
120. Ibid., p. 133.
121. Ibid., pp. 134-135.
122. Ibid., p. 167.
123. Ibid., p. 202.
124. Ibid., p. 290.
125. *Conchita. . .*, p. 58.

## Widow Roles — The Saints Show the Way

1. *Saint Elizabeth of Hungary*, by Nesta do Robeck (Milwaukee, Wisc.: The Bruce Publishing Co., 1954).
2. Ibid., pp. 90-91.
3. Martin-Maria Olive, O.P., *Praxedes: Wife, Mother, Widow and Lay Dominican* (Rockford, Ill: TAN Books and Publishers, 1987).
4. Ibid., p. 44.
5. Ibid., p. 68.
6. Ibid., p. 99.

7. Ibid., p. 103.

8. Ibid., p. 108.

9. Ibid., p. 134.

10. Ibid., p. 144.

11. Ibid., p. 156.

12. Ibid., p. 178.

13. *Angela of Foligno: Complete Works*, cited earlier.

14. Ibid., p. 17.

15. Ibid., p. 19.

16. Ibid., pp. 124-132.

17. Ibid., p. 125.

18. Ibid., p. 126.

19. Ibid., see pp. 367-368, note 12.

20. Ibid., p. 128.

21. Ibid., p. 129.

22. Ibid., p. 131.

23. Ibid., p. 138ff.

24. Ibid., p. 140.

25. Ibid., p. 142.

26. Ibid., p. 155.

27. Ibid., pp. 155-156.

28. *The Saints and Blessed of the Third Order. . .*, p. 72.

29. *Saint Bridget of Sweden*, p. 21.

30. Ibid., see Vol. II, p. 117.

31. Ibid., Vol. II, p. 43.

32. Ibid., Vol. II, p. 45.

33. Ibid., Vol. II, p. 47.

34. Ibid., Vol. II, p. 55.

35. Ibid., Vol. II, p. 86.

36. Ibid.

37. Ibid., Vol. II, p. 44.

38. Ibid., Vol. II, p. 45.

39. Ibid., Vol. II, pp. 256-257.

40. *Marie of the Incarnation. . .*, cited earlier.

41. Ibid., pp. 9-10.

42. Ibid., pp. 10-11.

43. Ibid., p. 51.
44. Ibid., see p. 11.
45. Ibid., p. 54.
46. Ibid., p. 56.
47. Ibid., p. 55.
48. Ibid., p. 16.
49. *Conchita. . .* , cited earlier.
50. Ibid., p. 118.
51. Ibid., p. 7.
52. Ibid., pp. 10-11.
53. Ibid., p. 20.
54. Ibid., p. 23.
55. Ibid., p. 24.
56. Ibid., p. 27.
57. Ibid., p. 29.
58. Ibid., p. 30.
59. Ibid., p. 32.
60. Ibid., pp. 44-46.
61. Ibid., p. 57.
62. Ibid., see pp. 59-63.
63. Ibid., p. 32.
64. Ibid., p. 73.
65. Ibid., p. 75.
66. Ibid., p. 104.
67. Ibid., pp. 104-105.
68. Ibid., p. 109.
69. Ibid.
70. *Rita: The Saint of the Impossible*, cited earlier.
71. Ibid., p. 16.
72. Ibid., p. 17.
73. Ibid., p. 18.
74. Ibid., pp. 19-21.
75. Ibid., p. 24.
76. Ibid., p. 32.
77. Ibid., p. 36.
78. Ibid., see p. 37ff.

79. Ibid., p. 42.
80. Ibid., p. 52.
81. Ibid.
82. Ibid., p. 56.
83. Ibid., p. 57.
84. Ibid., p. 67.
85. Ibid., pp. 71-73.
86. Ibid., p. 75.
87. *Rita: The Saint of the Impossible*, p. 102.
88. *St. Jeanne de Chantal...*, cited earlier.
89. *Francis de Sales...*, cited earlier.
90. *St. Jeanne de Chantal...*, p. 55.
91. *Francis de Sales...*, p. 3.
92. *St. Jeanne de Chantal...*, p. 88.
93. Ibid., p. 80.
94. *Francis de Sales...*, p. 62.
95. Ibid., p. 64.
96. Ibid., see p. 70ff.
97. Ibid., p. 231.
98. *St. Jeanne de Chantal...*, p. 103.
99. Ibid., p. 187.
100. Ibid., p. 189.
101. Ibid., p. 205.
102. Ibid., p. 211.
103. Ibid.
104. *Selected Writings from the Journal...*, cited earlier.
105. Ibid., p. 346.
106. Ibid., p. 98.
107. Ibid., p. 346.
108. Ibid., see p. 244.
109. Ibid., p. 246.
110. Ibid., p. 256.
111. Ibid., p. 248.
112. Ibid., p. 274.
113. Ibid., p. 279.
114. Ibid., p. 324ff.

115. Ibid., pp. 325-326.
116. Ibid., p. 344.
117. Ibid., p. 353.

## Jesus: The Second Bridegroom

1. *Angela of Foligno: Complete Works*, pp. 39-40.
2. Ibid., p. 123.
3. *St. Jeanne de Chantal. . .* , p. 185ff.
4. Ibid.
5. *St. Louise de Marillac. . .* , p. 188.
6. *Selected Writings from the Journal. . .* , pp. 109-110.
7. Ibid., p. 98.
8. Ibid., p. 99.
9. Ibid., p. 137.
10. Ibid., p. 229.
11. Ibid., p. 100.
12. Ibid., p. 135.
13. Ibid., p. 226.
14. Ibid., p. 258.
15. *Treasury of Women Saints*, p. 94.
17. *Selected Writings from the Journal. . .* , p. 297.
18. *Conchita. . .* , pp. 61-62.
19. Ibid.
20. Ibid.
21. Ibid., p. 63.
22. Ibid.
23. *Before the Altar*, by Concepción (Conchita) Cabrera de Armida, can be ordered from Sisters of the Cross, 1320 Maze Blvd., Modesto, CA 95351.
24. *Angela of Foligno: Complete Works*, p. 141.
25. Ibid.
26. Ibid., p. 142.
27. Ibid. pp. 142-143.
28. Ibid., p. 143.
29. Ibid., pp. 146-147.
30. Ibid., p. 148.

31. Ibid., p. 150.
32. Ibid., pp. 152-153.
33. *Francis de Sales. . .* , p. 4.
34. Ibid., pp. 138-139.
35. Ibid., p. 51.
36. Ibid., see pp. 78-81.
37. Ibid., p. 76.
38. *St. Louise de Marillac. . .* , pp. 169-170.
39. *Marie of the Incarnation. . .* , p. 63.
40. Ibid., p. 12.
41. *Selected Writings from the Journal. . .* , p. 173.
42. Ibid., p. 176.
43. Ibid., p. 143.
44. Ibid.
45. Ibid., p. 149.
46. Ibid., pp. 152-153.
47. Ibid., p. 153.
48. Ibid., p. 179.
49. Ibid., p. 357.
50. *Conchita. . .* , pp. 27-28.

### Mary: The Exalted Widow

1. *Angela of Foligno: Complete Works*, pp. 130-133.
2. *St. Louise de Marillac. . .* , p. 187.
3. *Selected Writings from the Journal. . .* , pp. 129-134.
4. *Conchita. . .* , p. 54.
5. Ibid., pp. 103-104.

Our Sunday Visitor's

# HOLDING HANDS WITH GOD

*Catholic Women Share Their Stories of*
*Courage and Hope*

Miscarriage, depression, breast cancer, abuse, divorce, addiction, and other specific, personal, chronic problems touch the lives of many Catholic women. While expert advice is plentiful, what so many women want is not the words of professionals but the comfort that comes from knowing that someone else has suffered the same struggles and has been able to find God in the midst of the storm.

**Holding Hands with GOD** provides that comfort.
A compilation of stories about pain and redemption, this is a woman-to-woman approach of personal witness.

**Holding Hands with GOD**
Edited by Ronda Chervin
0-87973-**577**-5, paper,
$7.95, 168 pp.

Available at bookstores. MasterCard, VISA, and Discover customers can order direct from
**Our Sunday Visitor** by calling **1-800-348-2440**.

Or, send payment plus $3.95 shipping/handling to:
**Our Sunday Visitor** • 200 Noll Plaza • Huntington, IN 46750

### OurSundayVisitor

Our Sunday Visitor Newspaper • The Catholic Answer • New Covenant • The Priest • Catholic Parent • Catholic Heritage • My Daily Visitor • The Pope Speaks • U.S. Catholic Historian • Christian Beginnings • Our Sunday Visitor Books, Tapes, Curricula, Software, and Offering Envelopes.
For a free catalog call 1-800-348-2440.

A79BBKCA

# Our Sunday Visitor's Family of Periodicals

**OUR SUNDAY VISITOR**
America's Most Trusted Newsweekly!

**CHRISTIAN BEGINNINGS**
A Resource for Early Childhood Religious Educators!

**NEW COVENANT**
The Leading Magazine of Catholic Spirituality!

**THE POPE SPEAKS**
For Thoughtful Catholics!

**MY DAILY VISITOR**
A Gift of Daily Inspiration!

**THE PRIEST**
A Perfect Gift for Your Parish Priest!

**CATHOLIC PARENT®**
Because You are What You Read!

**CATHOLIC HERITAGE**
Celebrates Catholicism's Rich Culture and Tradition!

**THE CATHOLIC ANSWER**
The Most Popular Question-and-Answer Magazine!

**U.S. CATHOLIC HISTORIAN**
Historical Parallels, Past and Present!

---

❏ **YES**, start my subscription to the magazines I have checked:

❏ Payment Enclosed    ❏ Bill Me

| | |
|---|---|
| ❏ Our Sunday Visitor | 1 yr. $29.95 |
| ❏ Catholic Parent® | 1 yr. $18.00 |
| ❏ The Catholic Answer | 1 yr. $16.95 |
| ❏ Catholic Heritage | 1 yr. $18.00 |
| ❏ New Covenant | 1 yr. $18.00 |
| ❏ My Daily Visitor | 1 yr. $ 9.95 |
| ❏ The Pope Speaks | 1 yr. $19.95 |
| ❏ The Priest | 1 yr. $35.97 |
| ❏ U.S. Catholic Historian | 1 yr. $40.00 |
| ❏ Christian Beginnings | 1 yr. $19.95 |

My Name _____

Address _____

City _____ State __ Zip_____

Complete coupon and mail to:
**Our Sunday Visitor**
Attn: Joel Harmeyer
200 Noll Plaza, Huntington, IN 46750
**1-800-348-2440**

A78PX14A

Prices are subject to change

Our Sunday Visitor...
# *Your Source for Discovering the Riches of the Catholic Faith*

Our Sunday Visitor has an extensive line of materials for young children, teens, and adults. Our books, Bibles, booklets, CD-ROMs, audios, and videos are available in bookstores worldwide.

To receive a FREE full-line catalog or for more information, call **Our Sunday Visitor** at **1-800-348-2440**. Or write, **Our Sunday Visitor** / 200 Noll Plaza / Huntington, IN 46750.

--------------------------------------------------------------

Please send me: __ A catalog
Please send me materials on:
    __ Apologetics and catechetics    __ Reference works
    __ Prayer books                  __ Heritage and the saints
    __ The family                     __ The parish

Name_____
Address_____Apt._____
City_____State___Zip_____
Telephone ( )_____
                                             A89BBABP
--------------------------------------------------------------

Please send a friend: __ A catalog
Please send a friend materials on:
    __ Apologetics and catechetics    __ Reference works
    __ Prayer books                  __ Heritage and the saints
    __ The family                     __ The parish

Name_____
Address_____Apt._____
City_____State___Zip_____
Telephone ( )_____
                                             A89BBABP
--------------------------------------------------------------

**Our Sunday Visitor**
200 Noll Plaza
Huntington, IN 46750
**1-800-348-2440**
OSVSALES@AOL.COM

---

*Your Source for Discovering the Riches of the Catholic Faith*